First World War
and Army of Occupation
War Diary
France, Belgium and Germany

47 DIVISION
Divisional Troops
Divisional Trench Mortar Batteries
1 September 1916 - 31 January 1919

WO95/2718/3

The Naval & Military Press Ltd
www.nmarchive.com
Published in association with The National Archives

Published by

The Naval & Military Press Ltd

Unit 10 Ridgewood Industrial Park,

Uckfield, East Sussex,

TN22 5QE England

Tel: +44 (0) 1825 749494

www.naval-military-press.com

www.nmarchive.com

Contents

Document type	Place/Title	Date From	Date To
Heading	WO95/2718 47 Div Trench Mortar Battalion Aug 16-Jan 19 (+ Nov 15-July 16)		
Heading	47th Division 47th Divl Trench Mortar Btts. Aug 1916-Jan 1919		
Heading	47th Divisional Artillery 47th Division Medium Trench Mortar Batteries 17th November 1915 To 31st July 1916		
Heading	War Diary Of 47th Division Medium Trench Mortar Batteries November 17th 1915-July 31st 1916		
Miscellaneous	47th Division March mortar Battalion		
Heading	47th Divisional Artillery 47th Divisional Trench Mortar Officer August 1916		
Miscellaneous	47th Division T. M. Batteries		
War Diary	Martin Piuch	01/09/1916	13/09/1916
War Diary	High Wood	13/09/1916	24/09/1916
War Diary	Drop Alley	25/09/1916	03/10/1916
War Diary	Eaucourt Front	01/10/1916	14/10/1916
War Diary	Behencourt	14/10/1916	21/10/1916
War Diary	Zillebeke	21/10/1916	31/11/1916
War Diary	Zillibeke Front	01/11/1916	30/11/1916
War Diary	Bluff Sector	01/12/1916	31/07/1917
War Diary	Ypres Front	01/08/1917	31/08/1917
War Diary	Ypres	01/09/1917	05/10/1917
War Diary	Appy Wood and Gavrelle Sector	06/10/1917	31/10/1917
War Diary	Arras Front	01/11/1917	30/11/1917
War Diary	Havrincourt	01/12/1917	31/12/1917
War Diary	Cambrai Sector	01/01/1918	28/02/1918
Heading	War Diary 47th Divisional Trench Mortar Batteries March 1918		
War Diary	Havrincourt Wood	01/03/1918	05/03/1918
War Diary	Ribemont	07/03/1918	21/03/1918
War Diary	Bus	21/03/1918	25/03/1918
War Diary	Mesulte	26/03/1918	26/03/1918
War Diary	Contay	26/03/1918	27/03/1918
War Diary	Mariely	28/03/1918	29/03/1918
War Diary	Herissart	28/03/1918	31/03/1918
Heading	War Diary 47th Divisional Trench Mortars April 1918		
War Diary	Martinsart	01/04/1918	28/04/1918
War Diary	Yvrench	29/04/1918	16/05/1918
War Diary	Millencourt	17/05/1918	29/05/1918
War Diary	Albert Dernancourt Sector	30/05/1918	31/05/1918
War Diary	Dernancourt	01/06/1918	30/06/1918
War Diary	Longpre	01/07/1918	14/07/1918
War Diary	Albert Sector	15/07/1918	31/07/1918
Heading	47th Divl. Artillery D.T.M.O. 47th Divisional Trench Mortars August 1918		
War Diary	Albert Sector	01/08/1918	31/08/1918
War Diary	Bouzincourt	01/09/1918	05/09/1918
War Diary	Montauban	06/09/1918	08/09/1918
War Diary	Mericourt	08/09/1918	09/09/1918

War Diary	Bellery	09/09/1918	20/09/1918
War Diary	Faux	20/09/1918	27/09/1918
War Diary	Fleury	28/09/1918	04/10/1918
War Diary	Radingham	04/10/1918	05/10/1918
War Diary	Radingham	06/10/1918	31/10/1918
War Diary	Pont A Chin and Froyennes	01/11/1918	11/11/1918
War Diary	Templeux	12/11/1918	30/11/1918
War Diary	Fouquereuil	01/12/1918	08/12/1918
War Diary	Labeuvriere	09/12/1918	31/12/1918
War Diary	Field	01/01/1919	31/01/1919

WO 95/2718 (3)

47 Div

Div Trench Mortar Batteries

Aug '16 – Jan '19

(+ Nov '15 – July '16)

47TH DIVISION

47TH DIVL TRENCH MORTAR BTTS.

AUG 1916-JAN 1919

@& 47th Divisional Artillery

47th DIVISION MEDIUM TRENCH MORTAR BATTERIES

17th NOVEMBER 1915 to 31st JULY 1916.

Army Form C. 2118

WAR DIARY

or

~~INTELLIGENCE SUMMARY~~

(Erase heading not required.)

Instructions regarding War Diaries and Intelligence Summaries are contained in F. S. Regs., Part II. and the Staff Manual respectively. Title Pages will be prepared in manuscript.

Vol 1 Top

Place	Date	Hour	Summary of Events and Information	Remarks and references to Appendices
			WAR DIARY OF 47th DIVISION MEDIUM TRENCH MORTAR BATTERIES NOVEMBER 17th 1915 – JULY 31st ~~[illegible]~~ 1916	

1875 Wt. W593/826 1,000,000 4/15 J.B.C. & A. A.D.S.S./Forms/C. 2118.

Instructions regarding War Diaries and Intelligence Summaries are contained in F. S. Regs., Part II. and the Staff Manual respectively. Title Pages will be prepared in manuscript.

WAR DIARY
~~or~~
~~INTELLIGENCE SUMMARY~~
(Erase heading not required.)

Army Form C. 2118

Place	Date	Hour	Summary of Events and Information	Remarks and references to Appendices
			47th Division Trench Mortar Batteries From November 17th 1915 to August 1st 1916. A summary of events from this date to August 1st 1916 is merely approximate as no record has been kept. Previous to this date No 7 2 inch Trench Mortar Battery No 8 1½ inch Trench Mortar Battery were Corps Batteries and remained in the line during an indefinite period. After this date No 7 & 8 TMBs became Divisional Batteries the personnel of each being composed of half RGA men & half Infantry from the 47th Division. No 7 TMB was commanded by Captain REES R.W.F. No 8 TMB by Lt J G Brown 10th R.F. the attached officer of the former being 2 Lt PARDEN Argyll Sutherlands	

Instructions regarding War Diaries and Intelligence Summaries are contained in F. S. Regs., Part II. and the Staff Manual respectively. Title Pages will be prepared in manuscript.

WAR DIARY
or
INTELLIGENCE SUMMARY
(Erase heading not required.)

Army Form C. 2118

Place	Date	Hour	Summary of Events and Information	Remarks and references to Appendices
			, of the latter Lt B. Burke 3rd Devonshire Regiment about Nov 16th both Batteries were sent to 47th Divisional School at LA BEUVRIÈRE. At this time there was some doubt as to the status of these Batteries; eventually at the School they were placed under the orders of the Commandant & in the line under the orders of the Brigadier whose Brigade front they were expected to cover. Rations were drawn from Battalions & each time Battalion & Brigade reliefs took place ration indents for TM Batteries were expected to be handed over, from Battalion to Battalion, & Brigade to Brigade which seldom occurred. Batteries worked in reliefs having rest billets close to the line, & relieved every 2, 3 or 4 days. Ammunition carrying parties were	

Army Form C. 2118

Instructions regarding War Diaries and Intelligence Summaries are contained in F. S. Regs., Part II. and the Staff Manual respectively. Title Pages will be prepared in manuscript.

WAR DIARY
or
INTELLIGENCE SUMMARY
(Erase heading not required.)

Place	Date	Hour	Summary of Events and Information	Remarks and references to Appendices
			~~was~~ difficult to obtain; the difficulties of keeping in touch with, generally, the Brigade H.Q. & the Batt H.Qs were overwhelming; the frequent non arrival of rations, & the long journeys in the line made the duties of a T.M.B. officer both arduous & harassing. On Dec 13th 15. Both Batteries went into the line with the 47th Division at VERMELLES, No 7 Battery being placed in the QUARRIES No 8 in the HOHENZOLLERN line opposite FOSSE No 8. During the 20 days in this position No 8 TMB fired approx 160 rounds at BIG WILLIE & the CHORD of which the greater number were fired on Xmas eve morning at 7 p.m. when a GERMAN MINE was exploded under the HOGS BACK. On January 4th both Batteries moved to the	these facts,

1875 Wt. W593/826 1,000,000 4/15 J.B.C. & A. A.D.S.S./Forms/C. 2118.

Army Form C. 2118

Instructions regarding War Diaries and Intelligence Summaries are contained in F. S. Regs., Part II. and the Staff Manual respectively. Title Pages will be prepared in manuscript.

WAR DIARY
or
INTELLIGENCE SUMMARY
(Erase heading not required.)

Place	Date	Hour	Summary of Events and Information	Remarks and references to Appendices
			Loos - DOUBLE CRASSIER post No 7 Battery being at the latter position No 8 at the former. On Dec 30th 2Lt C.W. KENYON 10 Lancs Regiment joined No 8 T.M.B & some days previously Lt W.N. Kirkland 5th P.O. Rifles joined the same Battery. After various ration & other difficulties No 8 T.M.B. installed themselves in the cellar of a house on the east side of Loos under Hill 70. Owing to the division front being shortened the guns which had been placed in position north of Loos CRASSIER had to be moved to the south side where they were placed in position; 2 guns near the CHALK PIT 2 guns in the COPSE (PENNMORE?). Up to February 14th about 250 rounds were fired. January 27th Lt J.J. BROWN went sick, was evacuated first to ROUEN; later till MARCH 5th	

1875 Wt. W593/826 1,000,000 4/15 J.B.C. & A. A.D.S.S./Forms/C. 2118.

Instructions regarding War Diaries and Intelligence Summaries are contained in F. S. Regs., Part II. and the Staff Manual respectively. Title Pages will be prepared in manuscript.

WAR DIARY
or
INTELLIGENCE SUMMARY
(Erase heading not required.)

Army Form C. 2118

Place	Date	Hour	Summary of Events and Information	Remarks and references to Appendices
			to the MICHELHAM CONVALESCENT HOME CIMIEZ. After coming out of the line, to LABEUVRIERE, Lt KIRKLAND on the 16.2.16 went sick, & was evacuated to ENGLAND, 2 Lt BURKE, on 22.2.16. was accidentally wounded by a bomb & was also evacuated to ENGLAND.	
			Lt C.W. KENYON about 8th January had ~~then~~ been ordered to report to a 15th Division T.M. Battery.	
			Lt B. St JH STORRS 45th Artillery Brigade Staff 8th Division on the 26th February came to No 8 T.M.B. On March 4th he was admitted to hospital with varicose veins & was later evacuated to ENGLAND. CAPTAIN REES then took command of both Nos 7 & 8 T.M.Bs, 2Lt KENYON, about the same period, returning as second officer to No 8 T.M.B.	
			On ~~February~~ MARCH 14th the Batteries went into the line on the SOUCHEZ - CARENCY front. MARCH 16th Captain REES was seriously wounded & 2Lt KENYON killed whilst	

Army Form C. 2118

Instructions regarding War Diaries and Intelligence Summaries are contained in F. S. Regs., Part II. and the Staff Manual respectively. Title Pages will be prepared in manuscript.

WAR DIARY
or
INTELLIGENCE SUMMARY
(Erase heading not required.)

Place	Date	Hour	Summary of Events and Information	Remarks and references to Appendices
			working 2 TRENCH T. Ms. 2Lt SCOTT 2nd Divisional Artillery Staff reported to No 8 T.M.B. MARCH 17th, Lt JG BROWN returning the same day to the Battery. Up to May 28th X47 Y47 T.M.Bs. as they were now called attached 47 Divisional Artillery took part in the usual bombardments & mine explosions of this period. About the month of April 247 T.M.B. was formed & the post of Divisional Trench Mortar Officer was created & filled by Captain WERNER R.G.A. the two subalterns of 247 T.M.B. being Lt R. HARDING 47th DAC & Lt H BOWDITCH D238 Battery, the three Batteries becoming from this time forward an integral part of respectively 235, 236, & 237, F.A. Brigades. MAY 18th A23 T.M.B. came into the line to take over the VIMY sector. Their casualties were unfortunately heavy & they were withdrawn after MAY 21st with less than half their strength. 2Lt B. PITT ~~[illegible]~~ BORDER REGIMENT had taken command of X47 T.M.B. about	

1875 Wt. W593/826 1,000,000 4/15 J.B.C. & A. A.D.S.S./Forms/C. 2118.

Instructions regarding War Diaries and Intelligence Summaries are contained in F. S. Regs., Part II. and the Staff Manual respectively. Title Pages will be prepared in manuscript.

WAR DIARY
or
INTELLIGENCE SUMMARY
(Erase heading not required.)

Army Form C. 2118

Place	Date	Hour	Summary of Events and Information	Remarks and references to Appendices
			MARCH 15th. This brave & valuable officer was lost in a mine explosion about APRIL 30th. Lt WHIDBORNE, 235 Brigade, took command of the Battery, the second officer being Lt JOHNSON 23rd Divisional Artillery. On May 29th the three Batteries were relieved & were billeted successively during the period up to June 13th at BAJUS, LA THIEULOYE, HOUVELIN & ANTIN. About June 7th Lt A. BROWNLEE succeeded Capt. WEBBER as D.T.M.O. On June 13th the Batteries went into the line in the SOUCHEZ - ANGRES sector opposite LENS. 2Lt T. FOLINGSBY 237 Brigade had previously reported as second officer to Y/47 T.M.B. 2Lt PROTT having returned to the 2nd Division Mortars. ~~From the~~ From June 13th - July 29th the 3 Batteries fired approximately 4500 rounds in wire cutting preparatory to raids & in general	

1875 Wt. W593/826 1,000,000 4/15 J.B.C. & A. A.D.S.S./Forms/C. 2118.

Instructions regarding War Diaries and Intelligence Summaries are contained in F. S. Regs., Part II. and the Staff Manual respectively. Title Pages will be prepared in manuscript.

Army Form C. 2118

WAR DIARY
or
INTELLIGENCE SUMMARY
(Erase heading not required.)

Place	Date	Hour	Summary of Events and Information	Remarks and references to Appendices
			retaliatory & offensive fire. ~~[illegible]~~ On June 22nd 2 Lt T. FOLINGSBY was killed whilst doing ~~useful~~ good work at the guns. During the day he fired over 120 rounds. 2 Lt MASSON 236 Brigade replaced him. July 1st Lt BROWNLEE after three weeks of unceasing work became ill & was later evacuated to ENGLAND. Previously Lt N BOWDITCH had ~~natural~~ been recalled to the wagon lines of his Brigade as the result of overwork & strain. Lt K HARDING most ably took his place at a difficult period & contributed very largely to the success of the 47th Division raids by his careful wire cutting & his unfailingly gallant conduct in the face of unfavourable circumstances & constant danger. He was seriously wounded about June 10th whilst firing one of his guns at night. Lt LATHBERT 239 Brigade	

1875 Wt. W593/826 1,000,000 4/15 J.B.C. & A. A.D.S.S./Forms/C. 2118.

Instructions regarding War Diaries and Intelligence Summaries are contained in F. S. Regs., Part II. and the Staff Manual respectively. Title Pages will be prepared in manuscript.

WAR DIARY
or
INTELLIGENCE SUMMARY
(Erase heading not required.)

Army Form C. 2118

Place	Date	Hour	Summary of Events and Information	Remarks and references to Appendices
			had previously taken Lt BOWDITCH's place. Lt HODGKINSON 237 Brigade took Lt HARDINGS place.	
			X47 T.M.B during this period made full use of its better position in the line & completely overcame German MINENWERFER fire in this sector. On June 17th the Battery fired 200 rounds in the course of 12 hours, demolishing much wire & parapets.	
			On 21st. 25th. 27th of this month the Divisional 2" T.M. B's fired for the first time as a unit along the whole Divisional front.	
			Lt J. WOOLLETT. 236 Brigade about July 7th took Lt Browns place in Y47 T.M.B, the latter officer having replaced Lt A. BROWNLEE as D.T.M.O. On July 29th, the Batteries were relieved by 63rd Div.	

1875 Wt. W593/826 1,000,000 4/15 J.B.C. & A. A.D.S.S./Forms/C. 2118.

Summaries are contained in F. S. Regs., Part II. and the Staff Manual respectively. Title Pages will be prepared in manuscript.

INTELLIGENCE SUMMARY

(*Erase heading not required.*)

Place	Date	Hour	Summary of Events and Information	Remarks and references to Appendices
			T.M.Bs. July 29. 30. 31st the Batteries were billeted in their respective Brigade areas, & moved by day by motor lorry as a unit. J.J. Brown Lt 47. D.T.M.O. August 27th 1916. NOTES. (1) Approx July 15. Lt TROLLOPE, 235 Brigade, relieved Lt JOHNSTON (X 47 T.M.B) who returned to 23rd D.A. (2) January 26th 1916. R.G.A personnel from St VENANT replaced infantry personnel, complete. ~~For~~ Nov. 20th R.G.A. personnel of Battery had been ~~[illegible]~~ returned to 1st Army T.M. School.	

Army Form C. 2118

Instructions regarding War Diaries and Intelligence Summaries are contained in F. S. Regs., Part II. and the Staff Manual respectively. Title Pages will be prepared in manuscript.

WAR DIARY
or
INTELLIGENCE SUMMARY

(Erase heading not required.)

Place	Date	Hour	Summary of Events and Information	Remarks and references to Appendices
			(3) Approx April 20th. 2" MORTARS replaced. 1½" MORTARS in Y 47 T.M.B.	
			[illegible] Lt.	

1875 Wt. W593/826 1,000,000 4/15 J.B.C. & A. A.D.S.S./Forms/C. 2118.

47th Divisional Artillery.

<u>47th DIVISIONAL TRENCH MORTAR OFFICER</u>

<u>AUGUST 1 9 1 6</u>

Instructions regarding War Diaries and Intelligence Summaries are contained in F. S. Regs., Part II. and the Staff Manual respectively. Title Pages will be prepared in manuscript.

WAR DIARY
or
~~INTELLIGENCE~~ SUMMARY
(Erase heading not required.)

Army Form C. 2118

Vol 10

Place	Date	Hour	Summary of Events and Information	Remarks and references to Appendices
			47th Division. T.M. Batteries.	
			August 1. Batteries billetted WAVANS. BEAUVOIRE RIVIERE district	
			" 2nd 5th / 3rd 6th / 4th 7th Rest. Took part in Field Battery manoeuvres.	
			August 4th Billetted PONCHEL - BOUFFLERS district	
			Inspection by C.R.A. on BOUFFLERS green.	
			Various attempts were made about this time to work T.M. Bs in conjunction with field Artillery in view of a possible moving battle. These attempts were comparatively unsuccessful.	
			" 8th 9th Rest & manoeuvres about BOUFFLERS.	
			Billetted at RIBEAUCOURT	
			10 11th HAVERNAS WARGNIES NAOURS.	
			12th T.M. B.Cs visited line in view of relief of 23rd Div. T.M. Bs	
			13th D.T.M.O visited line. Arrangements for relief made. Carried out Sunday [illegible]	

1875 Wt. W593/826 1,000,000 4/15 J.B.C. & A. A.D.S.S./Forms/C. 2118.

Army Form C. 2118

Instructions regarding War Diaries and Intelligence Summaries are contained in F. S. Regs., Part II. and the Staff Manual respectively. Title Pages will be prepared in manuscript.

WAR DIARY
or
INTELLIGENCE SUMMARY
(Erase heading not required.)

Place	Date	Hour	Summary of Events and Information	Remarks and references to Appendices
	August 15		X & Y/41 T.M.B.s handing over 6 guns to X & Y/23 Batteries, to replace 6 guns taken over from them in S.A.D. & S.2.C. Owing to the necessity of frequent reliefs, the narrowness of the trenches, the difficulty of ammunition supply & storage, the lack of suitable targets & our frequent local attacks on small portions of enemy trench, little could be done by medium Trench Mortars at this time, & the following system of work & reliefs was approved 1 Battery in charge of 4 guns 9 ORs 1 officer 24 hour reliefs Remainder of Battery living in shelters & dug outs at SHELTER WOOD 1 Battery " " of ammunition supply to the guns. 1 Battery in rest ALBERT. Batteries relieved each other every 4 days.	

1875 Wt. W593/826 1,000,000 4/15 J.B.C. & A. A.D.S.S./Forms/C. 2118.

Instructions regarding War Diaries and Intelligence Summaries are contained in F. S. Regs., Part II. and the Staff Manual respectively. Title Pages will be prepared in manuscript.

Army Form C. 2118

or INTELLIGENCE SUMMARY

(Erase heading not required.)

Place	Date	Hour	Summary of Events and Information	Remarks and references to Appendices
			Ammunition dumps were taken over at	
			CONTALMAISON 250 rounds	
			MAMETZ WOOD VALLEY W. SIDE 150 rounds	
			August 14th X Battery took over the line	
			Y " " ammunition	
			Z " ALBERT.	
			August 15th Fired 8 rounds on SWITCH LINE S2.A.5.2.	
			16th " 25 " " S.2.C.2.9.	
			17th " 6 "	
			18th 19th 20th Emplacement re-dug. About this time SWITCH LINE taken	
			up to BAZENTIN-PETIT – MARTINPUICH ROAD.	
			" 20th Y Battery relieved X. Z took over ammunition	
			21st 22nd Gun taken forward & emplacement dug behind SWITCH	
			LINE S 2 a 6.2.	

1875 Wt. W593/826 1,000,000 4/15 J.B.C. & A. A.D.S.S./Forms/C. 2118.

Army Form C. 2118

Instructions regarding War Diaries and Intelligence Summaries are contained in F. S. Regs., Part II. and the Staff Manual respectively. Title Pages will be prepared in manuscript.

WAR DIARY
or
INTELLIGENCE SUMMARY
(Erase heading not required.)

Place	Date	Hour	Summary of Events and Information	Remarks and references to Appendices
		August	23rd Battery emplacement dug in PIONEER TRENCH to fire on new switch trench S 2 B. 2. 8. D.T.M.O slightly wounded.	
		"	24th Z relieved Y Battery. X ammunition supply. Gun placed in position	
		"	25th New position completed in PIONEER TRENCH. BED brought up from old position	
		"	26th 8 rounds fired on S 2 B. 2. 8. Germans were seen to run.	
		"	27th 5 rounds fired on S 2 B. 2½ 5½	
			28th X Battery relieved Z Battery. Y ammunition.	
			29th X Battery fired 29 rounds on INTERMEDIATE TRENCH S. 2 D. 0. 7.	
			30th Heavy rain places guns temporarily out of action. Emplacement baled out & ready. German garrison of INTERMEDIATE TRENCH captured.	
			31st Work continued on emplacement.	
			End of month.	

[illegible] Brown Lt
[illegible] D.T.M.O. August 31st 1916

1875 Wt. W593/826 1,000,000 4/15 J.B.C. & A. A.D.S.S./Forms/C. 2118.

Instructions regarding War Diaries and Intelligence Summaries are contained in F. S. Regs., Part II. and the Staff Manual respectively. Title Pages will be prepared in manuscript.

WAR DIARY
or
~~INTELLIGENCE SUMMARY~~ X.Y.Z. 44th TMBs.

(Erase heading not required.)

Month of September 1916

Army Form C. 2118.

Vol XI

Place	Date	Hour	Summary of Events and Information	Remarks and references to Appendices
MARTINPUICH	1.9.16.	3 am	22 rds fired on BOTTOM TRENCH EAST and on cutting S2 A & B	
"	2 "	12 noon	A party of 15 Germans was seen to leave trench in haste on bombardment. Several of party were accounted for by machine guns & 2" Mortars	
"	3.9.16	4 pm	15 rds fired on cutting. Normal hostile retaliation of PIONEER ALLEY & vicinity	
"	4.9.16.	2 pm	11 rds fired. Heavy hostile retaliation on PIONEER ALLEY. Bomb. HARVEY wounded	
	5.9.16.		12 rds fired on S2 A & B.	
	6.9.16.		Quiet on front. Rain.	
	7.9.16		Heavy rain. No firing.	
	8.9.16.	6 pm	Fired 20 rds on BOTTOM TRENCH NEST. Slight retaliation.	
	9.9.16.		No firing	
	10.9.16.		5 rds fired. Rifle mechanism on No 2 gun out of action	
	11.9.16.		Visited 1st Division area preparatory to taking over. Heavy shelling HIGH WOOD.	
	12.9.16.		X.Y.Z. took over 6 guns in HIGH WOOD. 250 rds ammunition S.A.C. 5.A	
	13.9.16.		X. T.M.B. [illegible] returned to rest at D.A.C. Y & Z. took over guns in line	

2449 Wt. W14957/M90 750,000 1/16 J.B.C. & A. Forms/C.2118/12.

Army Form C. 2118.

Instructions regarding War Diaries and Intelligence Summaries are contained in F. S. Regs., Part II. and the Staff Manual respectively. Title Pages will be prepared in manuscript.

WAR DIARY
or
INTELLIGENCE SUMMARY

(Erase heading not required.)

Place	Date	Hour	Summary of Events and Information	Remarks and references to Appendices
HIGH WOOD	13.9.16		Preparations made for firing gas & HE during night. Operations cancelled.	
"	14.9.16		Preparations & orders received for firing. Again cancelled.	
"	15.9.16	6.20	Attack. Critical situation at HIGH WOOD dealt with by STOKES MORTARS. Immobility of 2" mortars which were required to fire on S 4 C 2.8 rendered them useless. Gunners LEWIS Rifled.	
"	17.9.16		Positions cleared, Amm: counted & stored.	
"	18.9.16		Guns dug out, preparations for moving forward.	
	19.9.16			
	20.9.16		Position of Battery. X line. Y. D.A.C. 2. carrying parties from X 29 D on MAMETZ - BAZENTIN LE GRAND Road.	
	21.9.16		Orders to place 2 guns in DROP ALLEY M 29 D 4½.4. 30 rds amm taken up by 2 T.M.B, 15 of which were gas.	
	22.9.16		5 rounds fired on FLERS LINE (Bülowstellung) M 29.B.	
	23.9.16		10 rounds fired on same target. R T.M.B carried up 25 rds 15 gas.	
	24.9.16		10 rounds fired same target. Retaliation on DROP ALLEY	
			30 rounds fired " .	

2449 Wt. W14957/M90 750,000 1/16 J.B.C. & A. Forms/C.2118/12.

Instructions regarding War Diaries and Intelligence Summaries are contained in F. S. Regs., Part II. and the Staff Manual respectively. Title Pages will be prepared in manuscript.

WAR DIARY
or
INTELLIGENCE SUMMARY
(Erase heading not required.)

Army Form C. 2118.

Place	Date	Hour	Summary of Events and Information	Remarks and references to Appendices
DROP ALLEY.	25.9.16	12.35 pm.	Attack. 1st Division bombed about 100 yds up FLERS line. GUEUDECOURT. MORVAL. LESBOEUFS taken	
"	26.9.16.	10 am.	Y [illegible] relieved X [illegible]. Latter returned to D.A.C. 17 rds fired on FLERS line.	
"	27.9.16.		3rd gun brought forward from HIGH WOOD. 2nd gun advanced up FLERS line to within 150 yds of bombing post M29D38. 1st gun original position DROP ALLEY	
"	28.9.16.		10 rds fired. 5 gas Bombs.	
"	29.9.16		50 infantry carrying party took up 25 bombs. 20 rounds fired.	
"	30.9.16		25 " 22 " 42 rounds fired in conjunction with Heavies against Bombing Post. Appreciation of infantry obtained, owing to frequent [illegible] of "Legions" & [illegible] shooting.	
	1.10.16		30 rounds fired previous to attack at 3.15 pm.	
	2.10.16		Heavy rain. Position obscure around EAUCOURT L'ABBAYE.	
	3.10.16	12 noon	X [illegible] relieved Y [illegible] 12 noon. Latter returned to D.A.C. Position at EAUCOURT L'ABBAYE [illegible] & possibility of moving forward considered ~~[illegible] [illegible]. Heavy rain~~	

2449 Wt. W14957/M90 750,000 1/16 J.B.C. & A. Forms/C.2118/12.

Instructions regarding War Diaries and Intelligence Summaries are contained in F. S. Regs., Part II. and the Staff Manual respectively. Title Pages will be prepared in manuscript.

Army Form C. 2118.

TM B 47 D

Vol 12

WAR DIARY
or
INTELLIGENCE SUMMARY
(Erase heading not required.)

October 1. - 31st

T.M. Bs 47 D.A.

Place	Date	Hour	Summary of Events and Information	Remarks and references to Appendices
EAUCOURT FRONT.	1.	3.15.	Attack by 1st Division on FLERS line. Fired 30 rounds previous to it.	
	2		No firing. Position obscure around EAUCOURT	
	3.		X TMB relieved Y TMB. Latter returned to DAC.	
	4		Heavy rain. Advanced guns down FLERS LINE short distance.	
	5.		Reconnoitred FLERS line. EAUCOURT L'ABBAYE & WARLENCOURT Hill	
	6		Amm: in HIGH WOOD cleared & stored. Orders to take 2 guns forward to WARLENCOURT Hill	
	7		Amm: dump of 70 rounds formed DROP ALLEY also dump at end of sap M22D. 70 rounds. Gas bombs brought forward from HIGH WOOD to QUARRY EAUCOURT L'ABBAYE	
	8		2 guns taken to M 17 D	
	9		Positions chosen guns registered from M17 D 6.0.	
			25 rounds taken to position. Heavy shelling during day	
			27 " " " by Z TMB	
	10.		X fired 10 rounds on enemy front line from M17 D 6.0.	
	11.		Orders for relief discussed with DTMO 9th Division	
	12.	1-4am	Attack by 9th Division. No gas bombs allowed to be fired. X47 TMB fired 20 rounds HE	
	13.		Relieved by 9th Division TMBs. X 47 TMB carried 26 rds HE to M17D before relief	
	14.	–	TMB rejoined D.A.C.	

2449 Wt. W14957/M90 750,000 1/16 J.B.C. & A. Forms/C.2118/12.

Army Form C. 2118.

WAR DIARY
or
~~INTELLIGENCE SUMMARY~~
(Erase heading not required.)

Instructions regarding War Diaries and Intelligence Summaries are contained in F. S. Regs., Part II. and the Staff Manual respectively. Title Pages will be prepared in manuscript.

Place	Date	Hour	Summary of Events and Information	Remarks and references to Appendices
BEHENCOURT	4 – 10.16	21	March table as for 44 D.A.C.	
ZILLEBEKE	21.	2 pm	44th T.M.Bs relieved 2nd Australian T.M.Bs on SANCTUARY WOOD front I24 c.d (ZILLEBEKE trench map) 6 2" Mortars 3 9.45 T.Ms taken over by Y44 T.M.B.	
	22	3 pm	44th T.M.Bs relieved 4th Australian T.M.Bs on BLUFF FRONT I34 and I28 5 2" Mortars 2 9.45 Mortars taken over by Z44 T.M.B & X44 T.M.B.	
	23	–	6 rounds by X44 T.M.B on registration of enemy crater I34 c 9.0. Australian TMB brought into line to reinforce	brought into line to reinforce
	24	–	4 rounds " " "	
	25	–	12 " " in retaliation for heavy MINENWERFER fire 67 by Y44 T.M.B in retaliation	
	26	–	15 " in retaliation for heavy MINENWERFER fire	
	27	–	69 " fired by X & Z T.M.Bs on destruction of enemy wire in front from I34 d 2.7 to YSER Canal	
	28		166 rounds fired on wire cutting & destruction enemy M.G emplacement I34 D	
	29		122 rounds fired wire cutting. Usual retaliation by MINENWERFERS & shells	
	30		310 rounds fired on organized bombardment of enemy works I34 D	
	31		40 rounds fired in retaliation. No 1163 Bombardier Gibbons & No 2356 DAVIES wounded by direct hit on gun.	

[Signature illegible]
44th Div.

2449 Wt. W14957/M90 750,000 1/16 J.B.C. & A. Forms/C.2118/12.

Army Form C. 2118.

WAR DIARY
or
INTELLIGENCE SUMMARY
(Erase heading not required.)

Instructions regarding War Diaries and Intelligence Summaries are contained in F. S. Regs., Part II. and the Staff Manual respectively. Title Pages will be prepared in manuscript.

November 1st–30th — T. M. Bs 47th D.A.

Vol 13

Place	Date	Hour	Summary of Events and Information	Remarks and references to Appendices
Zillebeke Front	1916 1 Nov, st	10 A.M.	Z Battery fired four rounds.	
			2 guns placed in position against anticipated crater I 35 A 3 9	
			reorganisation of line on withdrawal of II Australian T. M. B.	
			Beds & guns brought up by Y 47th T. M. B.	
"	1 Nov 2		Orders for retaliation & wire cutting cancelled.	
			Batteries reorganised X. T. M. B. with 6 guns under Right group Col Ely	
			Z. T. M. B. with 6 guns under Left group.	
"			Rounds fired in retaliation Z. T. M. B. 32	
			" " " " X. T. M. B. 0.	
			5 guns in action in X. T. M. B. front	
			3 " " " " Z. T. M. B. "	
"		6.30pm	200 rounds sent up line by D. A. C.	
	1 Nov 3.		Only retaliation ordered.	
			Z. T. M. B. ordered to knock out Minenwerfer	
			Arcs & Zones made out fresh on maps, marking new positions	
			Capt Barry wounded.	

2449 Wt. W14957/M90 750,000 1/16 J.B.C. & A. Forms/C.2118/12.

Instructions regarding War Diaries and Intelligence Summaries are contained in F. S. Regs., Part II. and the Staff Manual respectively. Title Pages will be prepared in manuscript.

WAR DIARY
or
INTELLIGENCE SUMMARY
(Erase heading not required.)

Army Form C. 2118.

Place	Date	Hour	Summary of Events and Information	Remarks and references to Appendices
Zillebeke Front	1916 Nov 4	3-PM	Left Batt front reconnoitred with a view to bringing up Y. T. M. B.	
			X. T. M. B. fired 28 rounds in retaliation	
			Z. do. " 36 " " destruction of wire	
			Cpl Goldsmith wounded at No 2 gun	
			Gnr Dewar " " " " "	
			" Crofts " " " " "	
	Nov 5		X. T. M. B. fired 31 rounds in retaliation	
		4-pm	Z " " 0 " " "	
			Reconnoitred personally left Batt front. some trench mortar activity	
	Nov 6		X. T. M. B. fired 40 rounds in retaliation + wire cutting	
		"	Z " " 67 " " " + " "	
			O.C. Y. T. M. B. commenced reconnoitring + work on positions commenced.	
			Personnel of Heavy T. M. B. brought up to Ypres to work under him	
	Nov 7	"	Work commenced. very wet + rainy. Carrying party from 141st	

2449 Wt. W14957/M90 750,000 1/16 J.B.C. & A. Forms/C.2118/12.

Instructions regarding War Diaries and Intelligence Summaries are contained in F. S. Regs., Part II. and the Staff Manual respectively. Title Pages will be prepared in manuscript.

WAR DIARY
or
INTELLIGENCE SUMMARY
(Erase heading not required.)

Army Form C. 2118.

Place	Date	Hour	Summary of Events and Information	Remarks and references to Appendices
Zillebeke Front	1916 Nov 8	11 AM	X T.M.B. fired 35 rounds in retaliation	
			Z " " 26 " " "	
			Work carried on in Hill 60 Sector. Positions inspected by Major Lord Gorrell	
	Nov 9		X T M B fired 55 rounds in wire cutting	
			Z " " 56 " " " "	
			Positions inspected by General & Major Lord Gorrell.	
			R.E. work began on dug out for officers	
			Spring found on KNOLL ROAD.	
	Nov 10		X T.M.B fired 99 rounds. Work carried on in Hill 60 Sector	
			Water cleared, H Pit ditch. R & self inspected positions etc.	
			Went to Div Arty in evening, stayed at Poperinghe the night with Lt WHITBORNE.	
	Nov 11.		Saw Col Ely reference handing over Ammunition supply to groups.	
			Working parties & bombs carried up previous night from Knoll Rd dump. Walked from Poperinghe in the morning	
			X T M B fired 74 rounds in straf on Bluff Sector	

2449 Wt. W14957/M90 750,000 1/16 J.B.C. & A. Forms/C.2118/12.

Army Form C. 2118.

Instructions regarding War Diaries and Intelligence Summaries are contained in F. S. Regs., Part II. and the Staff Manual respectively. Title Pages will be prepared in manuscript.

WAR DIARY
or
INTELLIGENCE SUMMARY
(Erase heading not required.)

Place	Date	Hour	Summary of Events and Information	Remarks and references to Appendices
Zillebeke front	1916 Nov 12	4 PM	X T.M.B. fired 54 rounds in retaliation	
			Z " " 6 " " "	
			Ammunition carried from Knoll Rd dump up to Cellar emplacement by Infantry	
	Nov 13		Ammunition etc handed over to Left & Round group by D.T.M.O.	
			Ammunition taken up to Knoll Rd position by Infantry.	
			X T.M.B. fired 57 rounds	
			Z " " 0 "	
	Nov 14		D.T.M.O. went round the line with General	
			X T.M.B. fired 30 rounds	
			Z " " 8 "	
	Nov 15		D.T.M.O. & Brigade Major inspected gun positions	
			X T.M.B. fired 20 rounds	
			Z " " 51 "	
	Nov 16		D.T.M.O. & Major General went round the line	
			X T.M.B. fired 25 rounds	
			Z " " 59 "	

Army Form C. 2118.

Instructions regarding War Diaries and Intelligence Summaries are contained in F. S. Regs., Part II. and the Staff Manual respectively. Title Pages will be prepared in manuscript.

WAR DIARY
or
INTELLIGENCE SUMMARY
(Erase heading not required.)

Place	Date	Hour	Summary of Events and Information	Remarks and references to Appendices
Zillebeke Front.	1916 Nov 17	10 A.M	D.T.M.O. granted 7 days leave. Lt Widbourne took over D.T.M.O.	
			X. T.M.B fired 38 rounds	
			Z " " 10 "	
	Nov 18		X " " 66 "	
			Z " " 16 "	
	" 19		Ammunition taken up to Knoll Rd dump by D.A.C	
			X. T.M.B. fired 47 rounds in retaliation	
			Z " " 4 " " "	
	" 20		X " " 76 " " "	
			Z " " 16 " " "	
	" 21		X " " 42 " " wire cutting + destruction of enemy lines	
			Z " " 0 " " " " " "	
	" 22		X " " 48 " " " " "	
			Z " " 0 "	
	" 23		X " " 48 " " retaliation	
			Z " " 0 "	
	" 24		X " " 11 " " "	
			Z " " 72 " " + wire cutting	

2449 Wt. W14957/M90 750,000 1/16 J.B.C. & A. Forms/C.2118/12.

Instructions regarding War Diaries and Intelligence Summaries are contained in F. S. Regs., Part II. and the Staff Manual respectively. Title pages will be prepared in manuscript.

WAR DIARY
or
INTELLIGENCE SUMMARY.
(Erase heading not required.)

Army Form C. 2118.

Place	Date	Hour	Summary of Events and Information	Remarks and references to Appendices
Zillebeke Front	Nov 25	4 PM	X T M B fired 8 rounds in retaliation	
			Z " " 10 " " "	
	" 26		X " " 14 " " "	
			Z " " 14 " " "	
			Ammunition carried from Knoll Rd Dump to position by Infantry	
	" 27		X T. M. B. fired 13 rounds in retaliation	
			Z " " 60 " " " & wire cutting	
	" 28		X " " 0 "	
			Z " " 0 "	
			Ammunition taken up to Knoll Rd Dump by D. A. C.	
	" 29		X T. M. B fired 0 rounds	
			Z " " 0 "	
	" 30		X " " 0 "	
			Z " " 28 " in retaliation	

[signature illegible]
a/D T M O 47 Divn.

2353 Wt. W2544/1454 700,000 5/15 D. D. & L. A.D.S.S./Forms/C. 2118.

Trench Mortar Batteries
47th. Divisional Artillery

Instructions regarding War Diaries and Intelligence Summaries are contained in F. S. Regs., Part II. and the Staff Manual respectively. Title Pages will be prepared in manuscript.

WAR DIARY
or
~~INTELLIGENCE SUMMARY~~

(Erase heading not required.)

Confidential

December. 1916

Army Form C. 2118.

Vol 14

Place	Date	Hour	Summary of Events and Information	Remarks and references to Appendices
Bluff Sector	1	-	Work continues on gun positions by all Batteries: rounds fired nil.	
"	2	-	Rounds fired nil.	
"	3	-	X47 TMB fired 18 rounds on wire in Ravine & Canal Sector	
			Z fired nil.	
"	4	-	Rounds fired nil.	
"	5	-	X47 TMB fired 39 in retaliation for hostile fire	
"	6	-	24 rounds fired by X & Z TMB	
			Rest Billet of X47 TMB moved to Right Group H.Q. from VANCOUVER Camp by order of D.A.	
"	7	-	X Battery fired 16 / 2 " " 6 in retaliation	
"	8	-	X Battery fired 4 / 2 " " nil	
	9	-	X Battery fired 4 " / 2 " " 6	

2449 Wt. W14957/M90 750,000 1/16 J.B.C. & A. Forms/C.2118/12.

Instructions regarding War Diaries and Intelligence Summaries are contained in F. S. Regs., Part II. and the Staff Manual respectively. Title Pages will be prepared in manuscript.

WAR DIARY
or
INTELLIGENCE SUMMARY
(Erase heading not required.)

Army Form C. 2118.

Place	Date	Hour	Summary of Events and Information	Remarks and references to Appendices
Bluff Sector	10	–	X Battery fired 11 rds Z " 38 Heavy hostile trench mortaring on Hill 60 sub sector	
"	11	–	82 rounds fired in all on Divisional front on wire cutting.	
"	12	–	Rounds fired nil.	
"	13	–	Digging continued on new positions.	
"	14	–	38 rds fired by X & Z in retaliation	
"	15	–	V47 TMB fired 7 rounds on Hill 60 and CATERPILLAR with good results. X47 fired 36 Z47 " 226 with artillery support Heavy retaliation	
	16		V47 fired 3 rounds on Hill 60 and CATERPILLAR 27 rds fired by Medium T.M.Bs	
	17		73 rds fired by " "	

2449 Wt. W14957/M90 750,000 1/16 J.B.C. & A. Forms/C.2118/12.

Army Form C. 2118.

WAR DIARY
or
INTELLIGENCE SUMMARY
(Erase heading not required.)

Instructions regarding War Diaries and Intelligence Summaries are contained in F. S. Regs., Part II. and the Staff Manual respectively. Title Pages will be prepared in manuscript.

Place	Date	Hour	Summary of Events and Information	Remarks and references to Appendices
Bluff Sector	18	–	6 rds fired wire cutting	
"	19	–	Rds fired nil. New position dug in BENHAM ROAD I 29 c 3.6½.	
			New position started in rear of METROPOLITAN LEFT.	
"	20	–	Work continued with working party from V44 T.M.B.	
"	21	–	Rounds fired nil.	
	22	–	No activity	
"	23	–	X44 T.M.B. fired 27 } 2nd Lt SANDLAND and BALLARD posted respectively to	
			Z47 " " 62 } X + Y T.M.Bs from D.A.C.	
"	24	–	Work continued on emplacements on Hill 60 Left SECTOR	
"	25	–	Lt WHIDBORNE Lt BOWDITCH on leave. Railway dugouts shelled Xmas eve.	
			No activity	
"	26	–	Rounds fired nil	
			25 rds fired by X 44 T.M.B. Hedge Row position drained	
"	27			
"	28	–	X Battery fired 25 rds on wire Z fired 38 rds on special target	
			pointed out by miners ~~on~~ CUTTING CRATER. Good results.	

2449 Wt. W14957/M90 750,000 1/16 J.B.C. & A. Forms/C.2118/12.

Army Form C. 2118.

Instructions regarding War Diaries and Intelligence Summaries are contained in F. S. Regs., Part II. and the Staff Manual respectively. Title Pages will be prepared in manuscript.

WAR DIARY
or
INTELLIGENCE SUMMARY
(Erase heading not required.)

Place	Date	Hour	Summary of Events and Information	Remarks and references to Appendices
Bluff Sector	29	–	Rds fired nil Work continued on emplacements	
"	30	–	Y/47 TMB relieved Z/47 TMB on Hill 60 Sector New position reconnoitred by Brigade Major for V/47 TMB. Lt Ayers in command Y/47 TMB 2 Lt Ballard posted for instruction.	
"	31	–	Rounds fired nil.	

J Moor Lt Gunner
DTMO 47th Division

Instructions regarding War Diaries and Intelligence Summaries are contained in F. S. Regs., Part II. and the Staff Manual respectively. Title Pages will be prepared in manuscript.

WAR DIARY
or
~~INTELLIGENCE SUMMARY~~
(Erase heading not required.)

Army Form C. 2118.

Y/44th Div. — 47 Div. Trench Mortar Batteries — January 1st – 31st 1917 — Vol 15

Place	Date	Hour	Summary of Events and Information	Remarks and references to Appendices
Bluff Sector	1.1.17.		Rounds fired nil. Work continued on Bensham Road & Metropolitan positions. Drainage.	
	2.1.17.		Y/47 TMB fired 30 rounds in retaliation. 2Lt Hellage posted to Y/47 T.M.B. in absence of 2 Lt Ballard attending course with 2Lt Darby at BERTHEN.	
	3.1.17		Rounds fired nil. Heavy rain. No activity.	
	4.1.17		Nil fired. Two-way platforms sent up. Nine 3 from each Battery. 2 Newton Reds returned from Workshop with 2 pieces.	
	5.1.17		Bombardment by H.A. & Div. Art. of enemy front line system from Knoll Road to I 29 D. 4. 6. & I 35 a 35. 65 to I 35 a 60. 45.	
			X TMB fired 12 rounds. 1 close. 4 duds on Hill 60 & CATERP. line	
			Y/44 TMB fired 55 rounds from 3.45 pm – 4.15 pm	
			X " " 52 "	
	6.1.17		Work began on concreting Bensham Road position. Rounds fired nil.	
	7.1.17.		18 pdr shoot in conjunction with T.M.Bs on wire on north side of SHOAT. Cupolas brought up. Concrete work finished. 6 rounds fired by V.44 TMB.	

2449 Wt. W14957/M90 750,000 1/16 J.B.C. & A. Forms/C.2118/12.

Instructions regarding War Diaries and Intelligence Summaries are contained in F. S. Regs., Part II. and the Staff Manual respectively. Title Pages will be prepared in manuscript.

WAR DIARY
or
INTELLIGENCE SUMMARY
(Erase heading not required.)

Army Form C. 2118.

Place	Date	Hour	Summary of Events and Information	Remarks and references to Appendices
Bluff Sector	8.1.17.	3-30pm	22 rounds fired by Y/47 T.M.B. in retaliation	
		6 pm	X T.M.B fired 6 rounds	
			Bensham Road position completed with cupolas. Crater O.P. reconnoitred. Ypres heavily shelled.	
	9.1.17		Metropolitan position destroyed. Work began on pit 50 yds to the right Bensham Road work continued. 1 gun in action	
			V.47 T.M.B fired 20 rounds in retaliation at 2.50 pm.	
			X " " " 42 " " " "	
			V " " " 20 "	
			Enemies Trench mortars very active. Capt Lord reported from 47 D.A.C for instruction. attached to X 47 T.M.B	
	10.1.17		Rounds fired by Medium Batteries Nil. V 47 T.M.B fired 3 rounds in registration on Canal Sub sector	
			Visited work done on Pits by moonlight	
	11-1-17		Work continued on pits in the afternoon by 47 D.A.C working party	
			Strafe on Hill 60 Subsector Y 47 T.M.B fired 30 rounds. No activity on Canal subsector. Bearings taken on dugouts in Boche lines for V 47 H.T.M.B	
	12-1-17		Operation order No 1 received for 2 days bombardment on 15th & 16th arrangements made for cooperation on A. B & C areas. 100 rounds per gun sent up. V 47 H.T.M.B fired 1 round in retaliation	
			X " T.M.B " 61 " "	

Instructions regarding War Diaries and Intelligence Summaries are contained in F. S. Regs., Part II. and the Staff Manual respectively. Title Pages will be prepared in manuscript.

WAR DIARY
or
INTELLIGENCE SUMMARY
(Erase heading not required.)

Army Form C. 2118.

Place	Date	Hour	Summary of Events and Information	Remarks and references to Appendices
BLUFF SECTOR	12-1-17		32 Reserve Bomb Dump blown up by enemy Trench Mortar Position destroyed.	
	13-1-17		47 D.A.C carrying party of 20 men moved 198 bombs during the evening to gun position	
	14-1-17		X 47 T.M.B fired 5 rounds registration.	
			Y " " " nil quiet day. Work continued on pit.	
			Metropolitan Lift gun put in position. 2 way platform placed in position in NEW. CELLAR.	
	15-1-17		X.T.M.B fired 9 rounds ~~from~~ in registration 4 from DRIVE position recently finished	
	16-1-17		Bombardment on Hill 60 + Canal subsectors	
			allotment of 100 rounds per gun for X.T.M.B	
			" " 60 " " " Y "	
			" " 40 " " " V.H.T.M.B.	
			X T.M.B fired 289 rounds	
			V " " 47 "	
			Y " " 51 " Y Battery had a great amount of trouble with Beds. All guns out of action during day through this. Firing from 10-15 AM — 4 pm interval 12-15 - 2 pm. Gunner Wilson wounded, otherwise no casualties. Heavy retaliation by the enemy during the evening.	

Instructions regarding War Diaries and Intelligence Summaries are contained in F. S. Regs., Part II. and the Staff Manual respectively. Title Pages will be prepared in manuscript.

WAR DIARY
or
INTELLIGENCE SUMMARY
(Erase heading not required.)

Army Form C. 2118.

Place	Date	Hour	Summary of Events and Information	Remarks and references to Appendices
BLUFF SECTOR	17-1-17		2 days bombardment cancelled	
			X. 47 TMB fired 16 rounds in retaliation quiet day on whole front. very much snow.	
	18-1-17		Heavy snow & mist Nil rounds fired by medium T.M. Batteries. work continued on Beds & emplacements. X 47 T.M.B. relieved by Z 47 TMB at 4 pm.	
	19-1-17		Nil rounds fired Frosty weather no retaliation needed.	
	20-1-17		Rounds fired nil. work continued on gun pits.	
	21-1-17		Rounds fired nil. 2Lt Martin posted Z 47 TMB. New pit started near 32 Reserve crater Situation Normal	
	22-1-17		Rounds fired nil. work continued on pits D.A.C carrying party took up stores. Situation Normal	
	23-1-17		2 days Bombardment started at 9-30 am.	
			Y 47 TMB fired 110 rounds on Hill 60 Subsector	
			Z " " " 125 " Bluff & Canal Subsectors	
			V 47 H. TMB " 6 " from left gun	
			" " " 18 " " right "	
			2 Lt Hellier & Gnr Hooper wounded by our own Shrapnel	
			Bombardment stopped at 4 pm Enemy retaliated on Cutting, Larch Wood, Marshall Wk & Dumps 12.30, 3 pm & 3.30 pm.	

2449 Wt. W14957/M90 750,000 1/16 J.B.C. & A. Forms/C.2118/12.

Instructions regarding War Diaries and Intelligence Summaries are contained in F. S. Regs., Part II. and the Staff Manual respectively. Title Pages will be prepared in manuscript.

WAR DIARY
or
INTELLIGENCE SUMMARY
(Erase heading not required.)

Army Form C. 2118.

Place	Date	Hour	Summary of Events and Information	Remarks and references to Appendices
BLUFF SECTOR	24-1-17		All quiet on the Front. Z.T.M. moved billet to Vancouver Camp	
	25-1-17		Nil rounds fired. Col. Lowe & Brigade Major inspected Y 47 TMB on Hill 60 sector also V 47 H TMB gun on Verbrandenmolen in morning. No enemy activity.	
	26-1-17		Z TMB fired 7 rounds. Work continued on pits	
	27-1-17		Z 47 TMB fired 32 rounds in retaliation	
			Y " " " 29 " " " & on Caterpillar & machine gun emplacements	
			V H " " " 7 " " " "	
			Enemy retaliated on Ravine & Cutting	
	28 "		Z 47 TMB fired 5 rounds in registration work continued on emplacements no enemy activity.	
	29-1-17		" " " 7 " " " " of 30 Reserve 2 Newton Beds sent up to [illegible] Dp	
	30-1-17		Y 47 fired 31 rounds work continued on emplacements	
	31-1-17		Nil rounds fired. Work continued on emplacements.	

B. [illegible] Capt for Lt. [illegible]
[illegible] 47th Division.

2449 Wt. W14957/M90 750,000 1/16 J.B.C. & A. Forms/C.2118/12.

1-2-17 to 28-2-17

WAR DIARY
or
INTELLIGENCE SUMMARY

(Erase heading not required.)

Trench Mortar Batteries 47th Divn. Arty

Army Form C. 2118.

Instructions regarding War Diaries and Intelligence Summaries are contained in F. S. Regs., Part II. and the Staff Manual respectively. Title Pages will be prepared in manuscript.

Vol 16

Place	Date	Hour	Summary of Events and Information	Remarks and references to Appendices
Bluff Sector.	1-2-17		Rounds fired Nil. work continued on emplacements.	
" "	2-2-17.		Rounds fired Nil " " " " " – D.T.M.O. conference T.M. School Adjutant Left Group visited gun position.	
" "	3-2-17		1-T.M.B fired 60 rounds on cutting	
" "	4-2-17		1 " " fired 36 " " 2 T.M.B fired 10 rounds, Bombr Emery & Gunner Brebner & Lewis KILLED in action	
" "	5-2-17		Rounds fired Nil Hard frost prevents work.	
" "	6-2-17		Rounds fired Nil New position started at WOOLLEY Walk by 2-T.M.B	
"	7-2-17		Rounds fired Nil. Hard frost prevents work.	

2119 Wt. W14957/M90 750,000 1/16 J.B.C. & A. Forms/C.2118/12.

Army Form C. 2118.

WAR DIARY
or
INTELLIGENCE SUMMARY
(Erase heading not required.)

Instructions regarding War Diaries and Intelligence Summaries are contained in F. S. Regs., Part II. and the Staff Manual respectively. Title Pages will be prepared in manuscript.

Place	Date	Hour	Summary of Events and Information	Remarks and references to Appendices
Bluff Sector	8.2.17		Rounds fired nil. Work continued on emplacements.	
" "	9.2.17		Shoot on wire 59 rounds fired on crater by X.T.M.B.	
" "	10.2.17		Rounds fired nil. Hard frost continues.	
" "	11.2.17		" " Work continued on emplacements	
" "	12.2.17		Y. T.M.B reinforced Right Group T.M.B. Expended nil. Gunner Lansome wounded.	
" "	13.2.17		X T.M.B fired 54 rounds on wire and trenches.	
" "	14.2.17		X fired 50 / Y " " 47 / Z " " 57 } Total 157 on wire and trenches salient I34 D & B.	

2449 Wt. W14957/M90 750,000 1/16 J.B.C. & A. Forms/C.2118/12.

Instructions regarding War Diaries and Intelligence Summaries are contained in F. S. Regs., Part II. and the Staff Manual respectively. Title Pages will be prepared in manuscript.

WAR DIARY
or
INTELLIGENCE SUMMARY
(Erase heading not required.)

Army Form C. 2118.

Place	Date	Hour	Summary of Events and Information	Remarks and references to Appendices
Bluff Sector	15-2-17		X T.M.B fired 65 Y " " " 100 Z " " " 89 } Total 254 on wire and trenches Salient I34D + B Ammunition taken to guns by D.A.C	
"	16-2-17		X T.M.B fired 91 Y " " " 65 Z " " " 122 } Total 278 " " " " Ammunition brought up to dumps by D.A.C. wagons	
" "	17-2-17		X/T.M.B fired 108 Y " " " 118 Z " " " 27 V/H.T.M.B 3 } Total 256 on hostile wire and trenches Gunner Fordham wounded Salient I34D + B	
" "	18-2-17		V/H T.M.B 5 X " " " 57 Y " " " 25 Z " " " 194 } Total 281 on wire & trenches Salient I34D + B	
"	19-2-17		Rounds fired 331 on wire etc Results very satisfactory	

2449 Wt. W14957/M90 750,000 1/16 J.B.C. & A. Forms/C.2118/12.

Army Form C. 2118.

WAR DIARY
or
INTELLIGENCE SUMMARY
(Erase heading not required.)

Instructions regarding War Diaries and Intelligence Summaries are contained in F. S. Regs., Part II. and the Staff Manual respectively. Title Pages will be prepared in manuscript.

Place	Date	Hour	Summary of Events and Information	Remarks and references to Appendices
Bluff Sector.	20-2-17		Raid on enemys trenches 140 prisoners taken. Smoke Barrage from Cellar Right, Caterpillar, Fir Lane, O.4.B, & Canal	
			X/ fired 9 smoke bombs	
			23 H.E.	
			Y " " 62 "	
			Z " " 24 "	
			V " 24 "	
"	21-2-17.		Z.T.M.B withdrawn from the line, expended nil, weather misty and wet.	
"	22-2-17		Rounds fired nil. D.T.M.O attends T.M. school. ammunition taken up to guns by D.A.C.	
"	23-2-17		Rounds fired nil. Dull & wet 400[?] handed over to 41st Div[?]	
	24		Rounds fired nil Work continued on emplacements etc	

2449 Wt. W14957/M90 750,000 1/16 J.B.C. & A. Forms/C.2118/12.

Instructions regarding War Diaries and Intelligence Summaries are contained in F. S. Regs., Part II. and the Staff Manual respectively. Title Pages will be prepared in manuscript.

WAR DIARY
or
INTELLIGENCE SUMMARY
(Erase heading not required.)

Army Form C. 2118.

Place	Date	Hour	Summary of Events and Information	Remarks and references to Appendices
Bluff Sector.	25.2.17.		Rounds fired Nil. Work continued on emplacements	
	26th		Expended Nil " " " " "	
"	27th		Expended Nil " " " " "	
"	28th		Y.T.M.B. fired 66 rounds in retaliation on S.O.S. call.	

[signature]

Capt. Gen List
D.T.M.O.
47th Division.

2449 Wt. W14957/M90 750,000 1/16 J.B.C. & A. Forms/C.2118/12.

Instructions regarding War Diaries and Intelligence Summaries are contained in F. S. Regs., Part II, and the Staff Manual respectively. Title pages will be prepared in manuscript.

WAR DIARY
or
~~INTELLIGENCE~~ SUMMARY.
(Erase heading not required.)

47th Div
T.M. Batteries
Vol 17

Army Form C. 2118.

Place	Date	Hour	Summary of Events and Information	Remarks and references to Appendices
	1917 March			
BLUFF SECTOR	1		X.47th T.M. Bty fired Nil Y.47th T.M. Bty fired Nil. Work carried out by Z.47th T.M.B building emplacements.	
	2nd		X.47 T.M.B fired Nil Y.47th T.M.B fired Nil Work continued by all Batteries on emplacements & Bomb Dumps Gunner Harris of X.47th T.M.B was Killed in Action	
	3rd		X.47 T.M.B fired Nil Y.47th T.M.B fired Nil Work continued by all Batteries on Gun positions ammunition recesses etc.	
	4th		X.47 T.M.B fired Nil Y.47th T.M.B fired Nil. Work continued on Pits etc.	
	5th		X.47 T.M.B fired Nil Y.47 T.M.B fired Nil. Work continued on positions etc.	
	6th		X.47 T.M.B fired Nil Y.47 T.M.B fired Nil. 288 rounds of 2" T.M. ammunition handed over to the 41st Div Arty.	
	7		Nil rounds expended. Work continued on pits & dug-outs Two pits begun by Y.47 T.M.B in PETTICOAT LANE. WOOLLEY WALK 32 RESERVE. Z.47 T.M.B finished 2 Pits in CRESCENT TRENCH.	

A6945 Wt. W11422/M1160 350,000 12/16 D. D. & L. Forms/C./2118/14.

Army Form C. 2118.

WAR DIARY
or
INTELLIGENCE SUMMARY.
(Erase heading not required.)

Instructions regarding War Diaries and Intelligence Summaries are contained in F. S. Regs., Par. II. and the Staff Manual respectively. Title pages will be prepared in manuscript.

Place	Date	Hour	Summary of Events and Information	Remarks and references to Appendices
	Mch			
BLUFF SECTOR	7	-	Work begun on 2 New Pits near GRAND FLEET ST. Cpl Goldsmith with D.A.C working party finished 2 pits in O.G. Line & one pit HEDGE ROW.	
	8.		V.47th H.T.M.B started new dugout near HEDGE ROW. Party from V.47th H.T.M.B under Cpl Goldsmith building dug out in Railway Embankment. Work begun on dugout at Farm I.28.C. X.47 T.M.B building overhead cover for BENSHAM ROAD position. Rebuilding dugout at LARCH WOOD. New parapet & trench built at CELLAR position. Y. Pit completed. Gun No 204 sent to X.T.M.B also 1 Newton Bed & elevating frame. Forward Bomb Dump started by D.A.C party at LARCH WOOD. All D.A.C. working parties withdrawn from T.M. for work on X. Scheme positions for F.A. Batteries. 1 Mortar No 214 sent by Z T.M.B to X T.M.B on Hill 60 Sub Sector. 1 Newton Bed & elevating from sent up from Bells to	X T.M.B

Instructions regarding War Diaries and Intelligence Summaries are contained in F. S. Regs., Part II. and the Staff Manual respectively. Title pages will be prepared in manuscript.

WAR DIARY
or
INTELLIGENCE SUMMARY.
(Erase heading not required.)

Army Form C. 2118.

Place	Date	Hour	Summary of Events and Information	Remarks and references to Appendices
BLUFF	March 9.		Rounds fired Nil. Work continued on pits.	
SECTOR	10.		2/Lt Oxley OC Z 47 TMB ordered to report to 2nd Army Arty School at TILQUES. Work begun on new position behind ALAN TRENCH by Z TMB. 2/Lt Martin to take command of Z 47 TMB. 400 rounds of 2" TM ammunition could not be brought away from Sunken Road Dump by 41st Div Arty on account of bad track & fatigue of teams. Cpl Brewer to bring down by railway 400 rounds from Sunken Road Dump. This order was sent by the Staff Captain to 47 DAC.	
	11		Rounds fired Nil work continued on pits etc.	
	12		Rounds fired Nil Work continued on pits etc. Bdr Browne of X.47 TMB wounded.	
	13.		Cpl Goldsmith's party relieved work continued on dugout. Rounds fired Nil	
	14		Rounds fired Nil work continued on Pits etc	

A6945 Wt. W11422/M1160 350,000 12/16 D. D. & L. Forms/C./2118/14.

Instructions regarding War Diaries and Intelligence Summaries are contained in F. S. Regs., Par. II. and the Staff Manual respectively. Title pages will be prepared in manuscript.

WAR DIARY
or
INTELLIGENCE SUMMARY.
(Erase heading not required.)

Army Form C. 2118.

Place	Date	Hour	Summary of Events and Information	Remarks and references to Appendices
	Mch			
BLUFF	15.		Rounds fired Nil. Work continued Z. TMB working party	
SECTOR			relieved.	
	16		Rounds fired Nil. All officers at Rest billets went to a demonstration	
			at T M School at BERTHEN. Cpl Goldsmith & party to report to	
			St Bowchetel to build Gun Pits for 18 Bty 235 Bde R.A.	
			2/Lt O'Malley joined T.M. & is posted to Y. 47 TMB for instruction	
	17		X TMB fired 8 rounds in registration Work continued on pits	
	18.		Rounds fired Nil. Cupolas & Iron Rails taken up to	
			X TMB by Bty Carrying Party.	
	19		Rounds fired Nil. Work continued on Pits etc.	
			Ammunition statements from Right & Left Group TMB forwarded	
			to Groups.	
	20.		Rounds fired Nil. Work continued on Pits.	
	21.		Rounds fired Nil. Work continued on Pits.	
	22		X TMB fired 30 rounds & Y TMB fired 19 rounds in retaliation	
			Work continued on Pits.	

A6945 Wt. W11422/M1160 350,000 12/16 D. D. & L. Forms/C./2118/14.

Instructions regarding War Diaries and Intelligence Summaries are contained in F. S. Regs., Part II. and the Staff Manual respectively. Title pages will be prepared in manuscript.

Army Form C. 2118.

WAR DIARY
or
INTELLIGENCE SUMMARY.
(Erase heading not required.)

Place	Date	Hour	Summary of Events and Information	Remarks and references to Appendices
BLUFF Sector	Mch 23		X TMB fired 30 rounds in retaliation Y TMB fired 16 rounds in registration. Work continued on Pits	
	24		X TMB fired 11 rounds. Y TMB fired 43 rounds on Hindenburg crater. V.H. TMB fired 7 rounds on Enemy front Line & M.G. emplacement with excellent results.	
	25		Rounds fired Nil. Work continued on Pits	
	26		Rounds fired Nil. Gunner Lovell of Z 47 TMB wounded	
	27		X. TMB fired 30 rounds in retaliation Y. TMB fired Nil. Work continued on Pits.	
	28.		X TMB fired 50 rounds in Retaliation Y. TMB fired 85 rounds in Retaliation. Work continued on Pits.	
	29		Rounds fired Nil. Work continued on Pits	
	30.		Rounds fired Nil. Work continued on Pits. Bombs taken up to X. TMB by D.A.C. Carrying Party.	
	31.		Rounds fired Nil Work continued on Pits etc	

S. C. Brown. Capt. Gen List
D. T. M. O.
47th Lon Div.

Instructions regarding War Diaries and Intelligence Summaries are contained in F. S. Regs., Part II. and the Staff Manual respectively. Title pages will be prepared in manuscript.

Army Form C. 2118.

Trench Mortar Batteries 4th Divisional Artillery

WAR DIARY or ~~INTELLIGENCE~~ SUMMARY.

(Erase heading not required.)

April 1917

T M Bty Vol 18

Place	Date	Hour	Summary of Events and Information	Remarks and references to Appendices
	April	1917		
BLUFF SECTOR	1.		X 4th T.M.B fired 26 in wirecutting, Y 4th T.M.B fired 96 in wirecutting. Heavy retaliation by the enemy no material damage done	
	2		X 4th T.M.B fired 21 in wire cutting on Bluff Sector	
			Y " " 53 " " " "	
			Z " " 88 " " " "	
	3		X 4th T.M.B fired 25 " " on Hill 60 Sector	
			X 4th " " 50 " " " Bluff	
	4.		All Batteries fired 265 rounds in all in wirecutting on Div	Front
			As a result of a premature burst of a 2" T.M. bomb	
			No 950358 Gnr Webb S T of X 4th T.M.B was Killed &	
			No 950490 Gnr Jones E of X 4th T.M.B was wounded	
	5		X 4th T.M.B fired 35 rounds in wire cutting on Hill 60 Sector	
			X 4th " 72 " " " Bluff	
			Y " " 118 " " " "	
			Z " 69 " " " "	

A6945 Wt. W11422/M1160 350,000 12/16 D. D. & L. Forms/C./2118/14.

Instructions regarding War Diaries and Intelligence Summaries are contained in F. S. Regs., Par. II. and the Staff Manual respectively. Title pages will be prepared in manuscript.

WAR DIARY
or
INTELLIGENCE SUMMARY.
(*Erase heading not required.*)

Army Form C. 2118.

Place	Date	Hour	Summary of Events and Information	Remarks and references to Appendices
	April 1917			
BLUFF	5		V.47 H TMB fired 12 rounds in wirecutting on Bluff Sector.	
Sector			The enemy retaliated very heavily with 5.9 & 4.2	
			No 96029 Cpl Quirch G of Z 47 TMB was killed in action	
			as a result of this heavy bombardment & No 45551 Gr Schofield AC	
			of Z 47 TMB was wounded.	
	6.		X 47 TMB fired 30 rounds in wirecutting on Hill 60 Sector	
			X " " " 24 " " " Bluff "	
			Y " " " 13 " " " " "	
			Z " " " 39 " " " " "	
			V. " " " 10 " " " " "	
			Y.47 TMB had a premature, with the result that	
			No 89669 Gr Oakley G was killed & No 95583 Gr Regan D.	
			was wounded	
	7.		The day of the Raid. In the morning Batteries fired	as follows
			X 47 TMB fired 48 rounds on Machine Gun Emplacements	
			Y " " " 14	
			Z " " " 14	

Instructions regarding War Diaries and Intelligence Summaries are contained in F. S. Regs., Part II. and the Staff Manual respectively. Title pages will be prepared in manuscript.

WAR DIARY
or
INTELLIGENCE SUMMARY.
(*Erase heading not required.*)

Army Form C. 2118.

Place	Date	Hour	Summary of Events and Information	Remarks and references to Appendices
	April	1917		
BLUFF Sector	7.	-	At 7-55 pm Batteries started firing Smoke Bombs with the result that a very excellent Smoke Barrage was put between our Lines & the enemy Lines.	
			X 47 T.M.B fired 23 Smoke Bombs & 12 High Explosives	
			Y " " " 15 " " & 23 "	
			Z " " " 28 High Explosives	
			V " " " 2 "	
			Lieut Martin, Gunners Gray G & Pte Thompson J of Z 47" T.M.B. were wounded	
			Cpl & Snowden of Y 47" T.M.B. was slightly wounded but this N.C.O remained on Duty & continued to fire his gun, for this act of Devotion to Duty this N.C.O was recommended for the Military Medal which he received at the hands of Lieut. General Sir T.L.N. Morland. K.C.B. K.C.M.G. D.S.O. commanding X Corps on the 29th April 1917.	

A6945 Wt. W11422/M1160 350,000 12/16 D. D. & L. Forms/C./2118/14.

Instructions regarding War Diaries and Intelligence Summaries are contained in F. S. Regs., Par. II. and the Staff Manual respectively. Title pages will be prepared in manuscript.

WAR DIARY
or
INTELLIGENCE SUMMARY.
(*Erase heading not required.*)

Army Form C. 2118.

Place	Date	Hour	Summary of Events and Information	Remarks and references to Appendices
	April	1917.		
BLUFF	8		X 4.7" T.M.B. fired 12 rounds in retaliation.	
Sector			Y. 2" V. Btty fired Nil	
	9.		X 4.7" T.M.B. fired 12 rounds in retaliation	
			Y " " 21 " " "	
			2 Lt. W. J. O'Malley Y.4.7" T.M.B. Killed in Action.	
			No 965074 Gnr Stevens J.C. died of wounds.	
			No 970051 Bdr T Binstead of X 4.7" T.M.B. slightly wounded.	
	10.		Nil Rounds fired. Snowy & misty weather.	
	11.		Nil Rounds fired work continued on building Pits etc	
	~~12~~		X 4.7" T.M.B. were relieved by a Battery of the 23rd Div	
			Z 4.7" T.M.B. relieved a Battery of the 41st Division.	
			X 4.7" T.M.B. returned to Rest Billets.	
	12		Nil Rounds fired.	
	13		D.T.M.O's Office moved from Railway Dugouts to Rest Billets at Vancouver Camp.	
	14		Nil Rounds fired.	

Instructions regarding War Diaries and Intelligence Summaries are contained in F. S. Regs., Part II. and the Staff Manual respectively. Title pages will be prepared in manuscript.

WAR DIARY
or
INTELLIGENCE SUMMARY.
(Erase heading not required.)

Army Form C. 2118.

Place	Date	Hour	Summary of Events and Information	Remarks and references to Appendices
	April 1914			
BLUFF	15		Y 47 TMB fired 30 rounds in retaliation	
Sector	16		Y 47 " " 30 " "	
			Inspection of Trench Mortar camp by Lt. Col	
			Allen H B Commanding 47th D.A.C.	
			Work started by all Batteries on building new	
			positions on the Bluff Sector.	
	17		Nil Rounds fired, Work continued on pits.	
	18		" " " " "	
	19		" " " "	
	20.		Y 47 TMB fired 6 rounds in registration.	
	21		Nil Rounds fired, work continued on pits etc	
	22.		Y 47 TMB fired 14 rounds in retaliation.	
	23.		Nil Rounds fired.	
	24		Z 47 TMB fired 22 Rounds in retaliation	
	2		V. " " " 7 " "	
			No. 58207 Gr Bedwell G J Killed in Action.	

A6945 Wt. W11422/M1160 350,000 12/16 D. D. & L. Forms/C./2118/14.

Instructions regarding War Diaries and Intelligence Summaries are contained in F. S. Regs., Part II. and the Staff Manual respectively. Title pages will be prepared in manuscript.

Army Form C. 2118.

WAR DIARY
or
INTELLIGENCE SUMMARY.
(Erase heading not required.)

Place	Date	Hour	Summary of Events and Information	Remarks and references to Appendices
	April 1917			
Bluff Sector	24.		110155088 Gr Lord W wounded. Both these casualties occurred as a result of a Heavy retaliation by the enemy.	
	25.		Wire cutting begun on Divisional Front from Ypres Canal to Railway Cutting.	
			Y47 TMB fired 116 rounds in wirecutting & on S.O.S.	
			Z " " " 73 " " "	
	26.		Y47 " " 24 " " " . Enemy retaliates with 5·9 & obtained a direct hit on Wooley Walk Ammunition Recess. 32 Bombs were destroyed.	
	27.		Y47 TMB fired 58 rounds in wire cutting	
			Z " " " 20 " "	
			110 59375 Cpl Harvey was wounded as a result of a premature burst of one of our Bombs.	
			The gun, elevating frame, 34 Bombs & 38 Boxes of Component Parts were destroyed.	

Army Form C. 2118.

Instructions regarding War Diaries and Intelligence Summaries are contained in F. S. Regs., Par. II. and the Staff Manual respectively. Title pages will be prepared in manuscript.

WAR DIARY
or
INTELLIGENCE SUMMARY.
(Erase heading not required.)

Place	Date	Hour	Summary of Events and Information	Remarks and references to Appendices
	April 1917.			
Bluff	28.		Y 47 T.M.B. fired 24 rounds in wirecutting	
Sector			Z " " " 10 " " "	
	29.		Y " " " 60 " " "	
			No. 114810 Gr Callender of Y 47 T.M.B. was wounded	
			No 11865 " Dallaway " " " "	
			No 940 493 Paskins " " "	
			These 3 men were wounded as a result of a	
			premature burst of one of our bombs.	
			No. 167788 Gr Elvidge A of V. 47 H.T.M.B. wounded by	
			Enemy Shellfire	
			Z 47 T.M.B. fired 10 rounds in wirecutting	
	30.		Y " " " 40 " "	
			Z " " " 10	

T. G. Moor[?]
Capt. Gen List
D. T. M. O.
47 Division

A6945 Wt. W11422/M1160 350,000 12/16 D. D. & L. Forms/C./2118/14.

Trench Mortar Batteries
4th Divisional Artillery

Instructions regarding War Diaries and Intelligence Summaries are contained in F. S. Regs., Part II. and the Staff Manual respectively. Title pages will be prepared in manuscript.

WAR DIARY
or
~~INTELLIGENCE SUMMARY.~~
(Erase heading not required.)

May 1917

Vol 19

Army Form C. 2118.

Place	Date 1917 May	Hour	Summary of Events and Information	Remarks and references to Appendices
BLUFF SECTOR	1st		Nil rounds fired, Enemy artillery very active Brisbane Dump blown up. 111. 9.45" Trench Mortar Bombs were destroyed, also 2. 2 way platforms for 2" T M & 1 platform for 9.45" T.M.	
	2		Nil rounds fired, work continued on pits & emplacements damaged by enemy Shell Fire.	
	3.		Nil rounds fired, work continued on pits etc.	
	4.		Nil rounds fired No. 970487. Cpl Goldsmith of V.49" H. T M. Bty was wounded today. This valuable N.C.O. was seriously wounded & it was with the deepest regrets that he heard he had died of wounds on the 6-5-17.	
	5.		Nil Rounds fired work continued on pits etc. In the evening the enemy started shelling the Trench Mortar Rest Billets at Vancouver Camp. 2 of our huts were destroyed & No 1646 Gr Michie	

A6945 Wt. W11422/M1160 350,000 12/16 D. D. & L. Forms/C./2118/14.

Instructions regarding War Diaries and Intelligence Summaries are contained in F. S. Regs., Part II. and the Staff Manual respectively. Title pages will be prepared in manuscript.

WAR DIARY
or
INTELLIGENCE SUMMARY.
(Erase heading not required.)

Army Form C. 2118.

Place	Date	Hour	Summary of Events and Information	Remarks and references to Appendices
	1917 May			
BLUFF	5.		of V. 47th T.M. Bty was wounded. At the time of the	
Sector			shelling this man was asleep in his hut. The shell	
			burst under the hut & blew him & his bed 20 yards	
			away. About 3 AM hostile shelling ceased & the camp	
			retired to bed again.	
	6.		Nil Rounds fired. Work continued on pits etc	
			The enemy again shelled the camp. The shelling	
			commenced at 11-15 pm & ceased at 3-30 am. Happily this	
			time no personnel or material damage was done.	
	7.		Nil Rounds fired, Work continued on pits etc	
			Heavy Strafe by our Artillery in retaliation ~~for~~	
			to his shelling of the previous nights.	
	8.		Nil Rounds fired Work continued on pits etc	
	9.		Captain J. G. Brown M.C. D.T.M.O. 47th London	
			Division, granted 10 days leave. His duties	
			were taken over by Capt. C. G. White O.C. V.47th H.T.M. By	

A6945 Wt. W11422/M1160 350,000 12/16 D. D. & L. Forms/C./2118/14.

Army Form C. 2118.

Instructions regarding War Diaries and Intelligence Summaries are contained in F. S. Regs., Par. II. and the Staff Manual respectively. Title pages will be prepared in manuscript.

WAR DIARY
or
INTELLIGENCE SUMMARY.
(Erase heading not required.)

Place	Date	Hour	Summary of Events and Information	Remarks and references to Appendices
	1917. May			
BLUFF	10.		X. 4.7" T.M. Bty fired 30 rounds on enemy's wire & trenches	
Sector.			Z " " " " 15 " " " " " "	
			Considerable damage was done to both wire & trenches	
	11.		Z/4.7" T.M. Bty fired 5 rounds on registration.	
	12.		4.7" Divisional T.M.B's moved Rest Billets from Vancouver	
			Camp to Camp at H.26.C.20.80. near Farm at Mille	
			Kapelle.	
	13.		Nil Rounds fired. Work continued on pits etc.	
	14.		No 951135. Bdr Cryer E.L. of Z. 4.7" T.M. Bty wounded	
	14.		Z.4.7" T.M.B. fired 31. rounds on enemy's wire	
	15.		Nil rounds fired. Work continued on pits etc.	
	16.		Z.4.7" T.M. Bty fired 47 rounds on enemy's wire.	
	17		" " " 21 " " " "	
			X. " " " 72 " " " "	
	18		X " " " 24 " " " "	
			Z " " " 21 " " " "	

A6945 Wt. W11422/M1160 350,000 12/16 D. D. & L. Forms/C./2118/14.

Instructions regarding War Diaries and Intelligence Summaries are contained in F. S. Regs., Part II. and the Staff Manual respectively. Title pages will be prepared in manuscript.

WAR DIARY
or
INTELLIGENCE SUMMARY.
(Erase heading not required.)

Army Form C. 2118.

Place	Date	Hour	Summary of Events and Information	Remarks and references to Appendices
	1917 May			
Bluff	19.		D.T.M.O's Office ~~fro~~ moved from Rest Billets at	
Sector			H.26.C.20.80 to Belgian Chateaux. A well known	
			Chateau partially destroyed. It is in the	
			close proximity of the well known & Historic	
			town of Ypres.	
			Y.47" T.M.Bty fired 25 rounds on Enemy's wire	
	20.		" " " " 58 " " " "	
			X " " " 43 " " " "	
			Z " " " 9 " " " "	
	~~21~~.		No 142922 Gr Hancock S. V.47" T.M.Bty wounded	
	21.		" 43290 Sgt Barrett A.E. Y.47" T.M.Bty wounded	
			" 956509 Gnr Maxwell T. V.47" T.M.Bty "	
			Nil Rounds fired	
	22.		No 57118 Gnr Clifford P. Y.47" T.M.B. wounded	
			" 27351 " Gregory G. Y. " "	
			Y. 47. T.M.B. fired 4 rounds. The forth round was	

A6945 Wt. W11422/M1160 350,000 12/16 D. D. & L. Forms/C./2118/14.

Instructions regarding War Diaries and Intelligence Summaries are contained in F. S. Regs., Part II. and the Staff Manual respectively. Title pages will be prepared in manuscript.

WAR DIARY
or
INTELLIGENCE SUMMARY.
(*Erase heading not required.*)

Army Form C. 2118.

Place	Date	Hour	Summary of Events and Information	Remarks and references to Appendices
	1917. May			
Bluff Sector	22		which damaged the gun pit & mortar. no damage was done to personnel of gun detachment.	
			X. 4" T. M. Bty fired 12 rounds on enemy's wire	
			Captain J. G. Brown M. C. returned from Leave.	
	23.		Z 4" T. M. Bty fired 50 rounds wirecutting	
			X 40	
			Y 30	
			A 2" T. M. gun at Grand Flat St position was destroyed by enemy Shell fire.	
	24.		X 4" T. M. B. fired 24 rounds on enemy's wire.	
			Y 35	
			Z 30	
			No 78019 Gnr Cox J.W. Z 4" T. M. Bty was wounded today.	
	25.		X 4" T. M. B. fired 36 on enemy's wire with satisfactory results	
			Y 34	
			Z 30	

Instructions regarding War Diaries and Intelligence Summaries are contained in F. S. Regs., Par. II. and the Staff Manual respectively. Title pages will be prepared in manuscript.

WAR DIARY
or
INTELLIGENCE SUMMARY.
(Erase heading not required.)

Army Form C. 2118.

Place	Date	Hour	Summary of Events and Information	Remarks and references to Appendices
	1917 May			
Bluff Sector	25.		The T.M.B's of the 8th Division reported to our Rest Billets today & became affiliated to us.	
	26.		X 4.7" T.M. Bty fired 34 rounds on enemy's wire with good results	
			Z " " " 30 " " " " "	
			The enemy retaliated heavily & we suffered a great many casualties.	
			Lieut. D. V. Ford O.C. X 4.7" T.M.B. was killed in action	
			Capt. C. G. White O.C. V. " " " wounded	
			No 18299. Sgt. Shaw J. V. 4.7" T.M.Bty. wounded	
			" 4100 Gnr. Murray A " " "	
			" 66 Bdr Ward C " " "	
			" 4447 Gnr. Murray A. " " "	
			" 1536 " Scott. A " " "	
			" 3513 " Smith R. " " "	
			" 166668 " Kitson W. " " "	
			" 956432 " Funnell R.C. " " "	

A6945 Wt. W11422/M1160 350,000 12/16 D. D. & L. Forms/C./2118/14.

Instructions regarding War Diaries and Intelligence Summaries are contained in F. S. Regs., Part II, and the Staff Manual respectively. Title pages will be prepared in manuscript.

WAR DIARY
or
INTELLIGENCE SUMMARY.
(*Erase heading not required.*)

Army Form C. 2118.

Place	Date	Hour	Summary of Events and Information	Remarks and references to Appendices
	1917. May			
Bluff Sector	26.		No. 906 Gnr Williams J. V.47" H T.M.B. wounded	
			" 2171 Rfm Rowe. S. X.47 T.M.B. "	
	27.		Z.47" T.M. Bty fired 30 rds on enemy's wire with good results	
			Y " " " 34 " " " " " " "	"
	28.		X.47" T.M. Bty fired 32 rounds on enemy's wire "	"
			Y " " " 30 " " " " "	"
			Z " " " 39 " " " " "	"
	29.		X " " " 79 " " " " "	"
			Y " "	
			Z " " 30 " " " " "	"
	30.		Y " " " 77 " " " " "	"
			Z " " " 118 " " " " "	"
	31.		Z " " 70 " " " "	"
			X " " 40 " " "	"
			No. 53294 Bdr Cole. H V.47" H T.M. Bty wounded	
			" 965918 Gnr Davey. F. V.47" H T.M. Bty wounded	Capt D.T.M.O. 47" Div

G.Brown.

Instructions regarding War Diaries and Intelligence Summaries are contained in F. S. Regs., Part II. and the Staff Manual respectively. Title pages will be prepared in manuscript.

June 1917

WAR DIARY
or
~~INTELLIGENCE SUMMARY.~~
(Erase heading not required.)

Trench mortar Batteries 47th Divisional Artillery

Army Form C. 2118.

Vol 20

Place	Date	Hour	Summary of Events and Information	Remarks and references to Appendices
BLUFF SECTOR	1917 June 1		X 47th T.M. Battery fired 41 rounds in wirecutting	
			Y/47 " " " 20 " "	
			Z/47 " " " 47 " "	
			V/8th " " " 30 " "	
			A great deal of damage was done by this firing to enemy's wire and trenches. Heavy retaliation followed	
			No. 956408 Bdr. F. W. Reynolds of Z/47 T.M. Bty was killed in action to-day	
	2.		X/47 T.M.B fired 42 rounds on enemy's wire + trenches	
			Y " " " 87 " " " "	
			Z " " " 20 " " " "	
			V " " " 40 " " " "	
			X/8 " " 75 " " " "	
			Y " " " 30 " " " "	
			Z " " " 40 " " " "	
			V " " " 60 " " " "	

Instructions regarding War Diaries and Intelligence Summaries are contained in F. S. Regs., Part II. and the Staff Manual respectively. Title pages will be prepared in manuscript.

WAR DIARY
or
INTELLIGENCE SUMMARY.
(Erase heading not required.)

Army Form C. 2118.

Place	Date	Hour	Summary of Events and Information	Remarks and references to Appendices
BLUFF SECTOR	1917 June 3.		X 47th T.M. Bty fired 103 rounds on enemy's wire + trenches	
			Y " " " 88 " " " "	
			Z " " " 52 " " " "	
			V " " " 24 " " " "	
			X 8th " " 169 " " " "	
			Y " " " 75 " " " "	
			Z " " " 79 " " " "	
			V " " " 60 " " " "	
			A great deal of damage was done to enemy's wire, trenches and Strong Points	
			In some cases the enemy was seen to leave what remained of his trench and run across the top. Enemy retaliated heavily with 5.9" and 4.2" shells but no damage was done to personnel or positions of T.M. B's.	

Instructions regarding War Diaries and Intelligence Summaries are contained in F. S. Regs., Part II. and the Staff Manual respectively. Title pages will be prepared in manuscript.

WAR DIARY
or
INTELLIGENCE SUMMARY.
(Erase heading not required.)

Army Form C. 2118.

Place	Date	Hour	Summary of Events and Information	Remarks and references to Appendices
BLUFF SECTOR	1917 June 4		X 47th T. M. Bty fired 93 rounds on enemy's wire & trenches	
			Y " " " 80 " " "	
			Z " " " 101 " " "	
			V " " " 40 " " "	
			X 8th " " 73 " " "	
			Y " " " 63 " " "	
			Z " " " 81 " " "	
			V " " " 62 " " "	
			Heavy retaliation with 5.9" and 4.2"	
	5.		X 47th T. M. Bty fired 76 rounds on enemy's wire	
			Y " " " 80 " "	
			Z " " " 87 " "	
			V " " " 7 " "	
			X 8th " " 91 " "	
			Y " " " 60 " "	
			Z " " " 82 " "	
			V " " " 50 " "	

T2134. Wt. W708–776. 500000. 4/15. Sir J. C. & S.

Instructions regarding War Diaries and Intelligence Summaries are contained in F. S. Regs., Part II. and the Staff Manual respectively. Title pages will be prepared in manuscript.

WAR DIARY
or
INTELLIGENCE SUMMARY.
(Erase heading not required.)

Army Form C. 2118.

Place	Date	Hour	Summary of Events and Information	Remarks and references to Appendices
BLUFF SECTOR	1917 June 5		A great deal of damage was done to the enemy's trenches and wire	
			Wire was practically demolished	
	6.		X 47th T. M. Bty fired 130 rounds on enemy's wire	
			Y " " " 90 " "	
			V " " " 83 " "	
			X 8th " " 70 " "	
			Y " " " 90 " "	
			Z " " " 80 " "	
			V " " " 77 " "	
			Wire passable in all places, but concertina barbed still remains	
	7.		The day of the great offensive of the 2nd Army against the Wytschaete - Messines Ridge. 1 2" Trench Mortar of Z/47 T. M Bty was ordered to go over the top with the 4th Infantry wave This Bty took 1 gun over to put it in second line of the enemy's trenches and fired 23 rounds on a Strong Point which was holding our infantry up. On completion of firing both	

T2134. Wt. W708—776. 500000. 4/15. Sir J. C. & S.

Instructions regarding War Diaries and Intelligence Summaries are contained in F. S. Regs., Part II. and the Staff Manual respectively. Title pages will be prepared in manuscript.

WAR DIARY
or
INTELLIGENCE SUMMARY.
(*Erase heading not required.*)

Army Form C. 2118.

Place	Date	Hour	Summary of Events and Information	Remarks and references to Appendices
BLUFF SECTOR	1917 June 7		Batteries assisted the R.A.M.C. in bringing in the wounded. Corporal Gibbons of 2/47 T.M. Battery was recommended for the Military Medal, which he received at the hands of Brigadier. General Whitley, C.M.G., commanding Royal Artillery of 47th Division. X 47 T.M. Bty was also ordered over the top. Through a misunderstanding this Battery arrived in the German Trenches before the Infantry; a hand to hand fight ensued Corporal Turner of this Battery who was in charge, his officer having been wounded, succeeded in killing one of the enemy and wounding another. The arrival of the Infantry relieved the situation. Cpl Turner then advanced to his objective but when he arrived there he found that the Infantry had advanced so far that his gun was out of range. He then returned to the wounded officer and with the aid of his detachment carried him through heavy shell fire to the Dressing Station.	

T2134. Wt. W708—776. 500000. 4/15. Sir J. C. & S.

Instructions regarding War Diaries and Intelligence Summaries are contained in F. S. Regs., Part II. and the Staff Manual respectively. Title pages will be prepared in manuscript.

WAR DIARY
or
INTELLIGENCE SUMMARY.
(Erase heading not required.)

Army Form C. 2118.

Place	Date	Hour	Summary of Events and Information	Remarks and references to Appendices
Bluff Sector	1917 June 7		This gallant N.C.O. was recommended for the Military Medal which he received on the 26. June, 1917 at the hands of Brigadier General Whitley, C.M.G. commanding 47th Divn Artillery	
			Sgt. T. Flanaghan was also recommended for the Military Medal for gallantry and devotion to duty. This N.C.O. had been doing very good work whilst preparing for the attack	
			This N.C.O. was decorated with the Military Medal by Brigadier-General Whitley, C.M.G., commanding 47th Divn Artillery on 26th June 1917.	
			2/Lt. E. J. Underwood, O.C., X/47 T M Bty was wounded to-day also 2/Lt. Campbell Browne 8th Div. T.M.B's.	
			No. 202778 Cpl Snowden, Y/47 T.M Bty was wounded.	
			965820 Gr Hammond, B. " " " "	
			148365 " Lewis, B " " " "	
			1545 " Hutson, J " " " "	
			166356 " Nilom, J " " " "	

Instructions regarding War Diaries and Intelligence Summaries are contained in F. S. Regs., Part II. and the Staff Manual respectively. Title pages will be prepared in manuscript.

WAR DIARY
or
INTELLIGENCE SUMMARY.
(Erase heading not required.)

Army Form C. 2118.

Place	Date	Hour	Summary of Events and Information	Remarks and references to Appendices
Bluff Sector	1917 June 8		All Trench Mortar Batteries withdrawn from the line to the Rest Billets at H 26 C 20 80.	
	9.		V/47 T.M. Bty have still 1 9.45" T.M in action	
	10.		The T.M. Batteries of the 8th Divn. were ordered to report to their own Division	
			The new 9.45" T.M in possession of V 47 T.M. Bty fire for the first time on the Ypres front.	
			4 rounds were fired with very successful results	
	11.		Nil rounds fired	
	12.		V 47 T.M. Bty fired 20 rounds on enemy's Strong Points	
	13.		V 47 T.M. Bty fired 8 rounds	
	14.		D.T.M.O's Office moved from Belgian Chateau to T.M. Rest Billets at H 26 C 20-80. near Farm at Mille Kapelle	
	15.		Nothing unusual occurred to-day	
	16.		47th Divisional Trench Mortar Camp moved from Mille Kapelle to Quebec Camp, Zevecoten	

T2134. Wt. W708–776. 500000. 4/15. Sir J. C. & S.

Instructions regarding War Diaries and Intelligence Summaries are contained in F. S. Regs., Part II. and the Staff Manual respectively. Title pages will be prepared in manuscript.

WAR DIARY
or
INTELLIGENCE SUMMARY.
(Erase heading not required.)

Army Form C. 2118.

Place	Date	Hour	Summary of Events and Information	Remarks and references to Appendices
Bluff Sector	1917 June 17.		Daily Training begun:- Reveille, 6.30 am; Physical Drill 7 am. Gun Drill 9.30 am till 12 also from 2.30 pm till 3.30 pm. Bathing Parades, etc.	
	18.		Routine of day's work as usual	
	19.		" " " "	
	20.		" " " "	
	21.		" " " "	
	22.		D.T.M.O. inspected Brigade parade at 9.30 am.	
	23.		Routine of duty as usual	
	24.		" " " "	
	25.		Capt. C. G. White returned to unit from Base and reassumed command of V 47 T.M. Bty.	
	26.		2/Lt. J. G. Blaver joined 47th Divl. T.M.B's from 47th D.A.C.	
	26		Brigadier General Whitley, C.M.G., commanding 47 Divl Artillery inspected the 47th Divl. T.M.B's and presented Military Medals to the following N.C.O.s	

T2134. Wt. W708—776. 500000. 4/15. Sir J. C. & S.

Army Form C. 2118.

Instructions regarding War Diaries and Intelligence Summaries are contained in F. S. Regs., Part II. and the Staff Manual respectively. Title pages will be prepared in manuscript.

WAR DIARY
or
INTELLIGENCE SUMMARY.
(Erase heading not required.)

Place	Date	Hour	Summary of Events and Information	Remarks and references to Appendices
Bluff Sector	1917 June 26		No 960295 Sgt Turner, L. M. B. X/47 T.M Bty	
			960318 Cpl Gibbons, J. S. Z/47 "	
			63975 Sgt Flanaghan, T. V/47 "	
	27		Routine of work as usual	
	28.		" " " "	
	29.		" " "	
	30.		The 47th Divisional T.M Camp was moved from Quebec Camp to Camp at M 5 D Central. All day it was raining heavily The camp was practically flooded and no tents arrived till 2pm. Eventually tents arrived and were put up and everything was settled	

J. B[illegible]
Captain
D.T.M.O.
47th Division

T2134. Wt. W708—776. 500000. 4/15. Sir J. C. & S.

Instructions regarding War Diaries and Intelligence Summaries are contained in F. S. Regs., Part II. and the Staff Manual respectively. Title pages will be prepared in manuscript.

Trench Mortar Batteries 47th Divisional Artillery

WAR DIARY
~~or~~
~~INTELLIGENCE~~ SUMMARY.
(Erase heading not required.)

July 1917

VA 21

Army Form C. 2118.

Place	Date	Hour	Summary of Events and Information	Remarks and references to Appendices
BLUFF SECTOR	1917 July 1st		Routine of work & training carried out as usual.	
	2.		" " " " " "	
	3		" " " " " " "	
	4.		Part of 47th Divl. T. Mortars camp at M.5.D. Central moved to 41st Div T. M's camp at H 31. D. 9. 1.	
	5.		Remainder of camp moved to 41st Div T. M. Camp. Guns stores etc, handed over by D. T. M. O. 41st Div to D. T. M. O. 47th Divl.	
	6.		Routine of training carried out as usual.	
	7		" " " " " " "	
	8		" " " " " " " 7. 6" Newton Mortars received. 1. 9.45" T. M. sent away. 6 2" T.M.	
	9		Routine of training carried out as usual.	
	10		" " " " " " "	
	11		" " " " "	
	12		" " " " "	

Instructions regarding War Diaries and Intelligence Summaries are contained in F. S. Regs., Par. II, and the Staff Manual respectively. Title pages will be prepared in manuscript.

WAR DIARY
or
INTELLIGENCE SUMMARY.
(*Erase heading not required.*)

2

Army Form C. 2118.

Place	Date	Hour	Summary of Events and Information	Remarks and references to Appendices
Bluff Sector.	July 13.		Routine of training carried out as usual	
	14		" " " "	
	15		" " " "	
	16		" " " "	
	17		The Rest Camp of the 47th Divisional Trench Mortars was inspected today by Brigadier General Whitley commanding the 47th Divisional Artillery.	
	18		Routine of training carried out as usual.	
	19		3. 6" Newton Mortars complete sent to 9th Corps.	
			1 " " " " " 41st Div T. Mortars.	
	20		Y & Z 47th T. M. Bs sent up the line to build 6" Newton Mortar pits for 41st Div T. Ms.	
	21		All Batteries sent up the line on ammunition carrying fatigue	
	22		" " " " " " " "	

A6945 Wt. W11422/M1160 350,000 12/16 D. D. & L. Forms/C./2118/14.

Instructions regarding War Diaries and Intelligence Summaries are contained in F. S. Regs., Par. II, and the Staff Manual respectively. Title pages will be prepared in manuscript.

WAR DIARY 3
or
INTELLIGENCE SUMMARY.
(*Erase heading not required.*)

Army Form C. 2118.

Place	Date	Hour	Summary of Events and Information	Remarks and references to Appendices
Bluff Sector	July 23.		47th Divl. T. M. Rest Camp & all 9.45" & 6" T. Ms handed over to 41st D. T. M. Bs.	
			47 Div T M B moved by Motor Lorries to a new Camp at R.15.A.0.4. between Boeschepe & Mt des ~~Câtos~~ Cats.	
	24		Routine of training carried out as usual.	
	25		" " " " "	
	26		" " " " "	
	27		" " " " "	
	28		" " " " "	
	29		" " " " "	
	30		" " " " "	
	31.		" " " " "	

[illegible signature]
Captain. Gen. List.
D. T. M. O.
47th Division.

A6945 Wt. W11422/M1160 350,000 12/16 D. D. & L. Forms/C./2118/14.

Trench Mortar Batteries 47th. Divisional Artillery

Instructions regarding War Diaries and Intelligence Summaries are contained in F. S. Regs., Par. II. and the Staff Manual respectively. Title pages will be prepared in manuscript.

WAR DIARY ~~or~~ ~~INTELLIGENCE~~ ~~SUMMARY.~~

(Erase heading not required.)

August 1917

Army Form C. 2118.

I

Vol 22

Place	Date	Hour	Summary of Events and Information	Remarks and references to Appendices
YPRES. Front.	Aug 1.		Training carried out as usual	
	2		" " " "	
	3		" " " "	
	4		" " " "	
	5		" " " "	
	6		" " " "	
	7		" " " "	
	8		" " " "	
	9		" " " "	
	10		" " " "	
	11		" " " "	
	12		" " " "	
	13		" " " "	
	14		" " " "	
	15		10 men from X. 47th T. M. B. attached to 235 Bde R. F. A. for Gun pit building	

A6945 Wt. W11422/M1160 350,000 12/16 D. D. & L. Forms/C./2118/14.

Army Form C. 2118.

Instructions regarding War Diaries and Intelligence Summaries are contained in F. S. Regs., Part II. and the Staff Manual respectively. Title pages will be prepared in manuscript.

WAR DIARY
or
INTELLIGENCE SUMMARY.
(Erase heading not required.)

II

Place	Date	Hour	Summary of Events and Information	Remarks and references to Appendices
Ypres Front.	Aug 15.		10. men from Y 47th T.M.B. attached to 236 Bou R.F.A. for Gun pit building	
			24 men from V. 47th T.M.B. attached to 41st Div. Ammunition Refilling Dump for duty.	
	16		Training carried on as usual	
	17		" " " "	
	18		" " " "	
	19		" " " "	
	20		" " "	
	21		" " " "	
	22		" " "	
	33.		10 men from ~~Z~~ 47th T.M.B. relieved the 10 men of X. 47th T.M.B. attached to 235 Bou R.F.A.	
	24		Training carried on as usual	
	25		" " " "	
	26		" " " "	

Instructions regarding War Diaries and Intelligence Summaries are contained in F. S. Regs., Par. II. and the Staff Manual respectively. Title pages will be prepared in manuscript.

WAR DIARY
or
INTELLIGENCE SUMMARY.
(Erase heading not required.)

Army Form C. 2118.

III

Place	Date	Hour	Summary of Events and Information	Remarks and references to Appendices
Ypres Front	Aug 27.		The 10 men of Y 47" T.M.B attached to 236 Bde F.A. & 10 men of Z 47" T.M.B attached to 236 Bde F.A & 24 men of V.47" T.M.B attached to 41st Div A.R.P. returned to camp.	
	28		Training carried on as usual	
	29		" " " "	
	30.		Camp of 47" Divisional Trench Mortars moved from R.15.A.0.4. at au Mont de Boeschepe to H 13 C 6.5. near village of Brandhoek. 4 9.45" T Mortars & 3. 6" Newton Mortars taken over from 8th Divisional Trench Mortars.	
	31.		24 men attached to Capt Warburton 47 Div Salvage Office to assist in salvaging guns etc. 24 men attached to O.C. Brisbane Dump to assist in ammunition work. 1 Officer & 10 men attached to O.C. "C" Group	

Instructions regarding War Diaries and Intelligence Summaries are contained in F. S. Regs., Part II, and the Staff Manual respectively. Title pages will be prepared in manuscript.

WAR DIARY
or
INTELLIGENCE SUMMARY.
(Erase heading not required.)

Army Form C. 2118.

IV

Place	Date	Hour	Summary of Events and Information	Remarks and references to Appendices
Ypres Front	Aug 31.		contd R. F. A to assist in Gun pit building etc	
			J. S. Brown	
			Captain	
			D. G. M. O. 47th (London) Division	

A6945 Wt. W11422/M1160 350,000 12/16 D. D. & L. Forms/C./2118/14.

Instructions regarding War Diaries and Intelligence Summaries are contained in F. S. Regs., Part II, and the Staff Manual respectively. Title pages will be prepared in manuscript.

47th Divl Arty. Trench Mortar Batteries

WAR DIARY
or
~~INTELLIGENCE SUMMARY~~.
(Erase heading not required.)

September 1917

Army Form C. 2118.

Vol 23

Place	Date	Hour	Summary of Events and Information	Remarks and references to Appendices
YPRES.	1/9/17.		Training carried out as usual	
	2		"	
	3		"	
	4.		1 Officer & 15. OR's attached for duty to Capt Warburton officer i/c Divisional Salvage Co	
	5.		T. M Camp moved from H.2.C.6.5. near Brandhoek to G.22.D. near Vauxhall.	
	6.		20 men attached for duty to officer i/c Cordova Dump.	
	7.		1 Officer & 20 men attached to 236 Bde HQ F.A. for work	
	8		Nothing unusual occurred	
	9		"	
	10		All Officers & men attached to other units returned to camp	
	11.		5 Officers & 119 OR's. attached for duty to 19th Div Arty. reserve camp	
	12.		47th Divisional Trench Mortar Camp moved from	

A6945 Wt. W11422/M1160 350,000 12/16 D. D. & L. Forms/C./2118/14.

Army Form C. 2118.

Instructions regarding War Diaries and Intelligence Summaries are contained in F. S. Regs., Par. II. and the Staff Manual respectively. Title pages will be prepared in manuscript.

~~I~~ 2 WAR DIARY
or
INTELLIGENCE SUMMARY.
(*Erase heading not required.*)

Place	Date	Hour	Summary of Events and Information	Remarks and references to Appendices
	Sept.			
YPRES	12.		G.22.D near Vaux hall to N.24.A.6.3. near Locre.	
	13		Nothing unusual occurred	
	14		" " "	
	15.		" " "	
	16		" " "	
	17		" " "	
	18		" " "	
	19		" " "	
	20		" " "	
	21		" " "	
	22		" " "	
	23		" " "	
	24		" " "	
	25		" " "	
	26		" " "	
	27		" "	

3

Instructions regarding War Diaries and Intelligence Summaries are contained in F. S. Regs., Par. II, and the Staff Manual respectively. Title pages will be prepared in manuscript.

WAR DIARY
or
INTELLIGENCE SUMMARY.
(Erase heading not required.)

Army Form C. 2118.

Place	Date (Sept)	Hour	Summary of Events and Information	Remarks and references to Appendices
YPRES.	28.		Nothing unusual occurred	
	29.		Operation Order received from 47 D.A.H.Q.	
			47 T.M.Bs will move by 10 Lorries on the 30th	
			to ROCLINCOURT near Arras	
	30.		1st day of move, route taken Hazebrouck	
			St Venant Lillers Bethune, stopped the	
			night at billets in village of Agnières.	
			[illegible]	
			Captain	
			D.T.M.O. 47th Division	

A6945 Wt. W11422/M1160 350,000 12/16 D. D. & L. Forms/C./2118/14.

47 DTM Bt
(1)
Vol 24

Army Form C. 2118.

WAR DIARY
or
INTELLIGENCE SUMMARY.
(Erase heading not required.)

Instructions regarding War Diaries and Intelligence Summaries are contained in F. S. Regs., Par. II. and the Staff Manual respectively. Title pages will be prepared in manuscript.

Place	Date	Hour	Summary of Events and Information	Remarks and references to Appendices
	[illegible]			
	1.		Arrived by Motor lorries from Ypres to village of Agnières where we stayed in billets 1 night.	
	2.		Moved from Agnières by Motor lorries to Camp near Roclincourt. Y & Z. 47th T.M. Bts. moved into the line in Oppy Wood & Gavrelle Sectors & took guns etc over from 63 R.N. Div.	
	3.		Arrangements made with Div. Train Officer for rations to go up by rail to T.M. Batteries in Oppy Wood & Gavrelle.	
	4.		22 rounds were fired by Z 47 T.M.B. on enemy's wire & trenches, satisfactory results were obtained.	
	5.		Work started on new pits.	

A6945 Wt. W11422/M1160 350,000 12/16 D. D. & L. Forms/C./2118/14.

Instructions regarding War Diaries and Intelligence Summaries are contained in F. S. Regs., Part II. and the Staff Manual respectively. Title pages will be prepared in manuscript.

WAR DIARY
or
INTELLIGENCE SUMMARY.
(Erase heading not required.)

Army Form C. 2118.

(2)

Place	Date	Hour	Summary of Events and Information	Remarks and references to Appendices
Oppy Wood & Gavrelle Sectors	Dec 6.		Work continued on new pits	
	7		do do do do	
	8		do do do do	
	9.		2 rounds fired by Z 4" T.M.B. in retaliation.	
	10.		Work continued on new pits	
	11		do do do do	
	12.		2 rounds fired by Z 4" T.M.B. in retaliation	
	13.		45 rounds fired by Y 4" T.M.B. on enemy's trenches & dump of heavy bombs was destroyed. Slight retaliation by the enemy.	
	14.		Work continued on new pits.	
	15.		35 rounds fired by Z 4" T.M. Bty on enemy's wire.	
	16.		33 rounds fired by Y 4" T.M. Bty on enemy's	

Instructions regarding War Diaries and Intelligence Summaries are contained in F. S. Regs., Part II. and the Staff Manual respectively. Title pages will be prepared in manuscript.

Army Form C. 2118.

WAR DIARY
or
INTELLIGENCE SUMMARY.
(*Erase heading not required.*)

3

Place	Date	Hour	Summary of Events and Information	Remarks and references to Appendices
	October			
Opper				
Wood &	15.		wire & trenches, a bomb dump was	
Gavrelle			destroyed, slight retaliation by the enemy.	
Sectors	17.		32 rounds fired by Y. 47" T M Bty on enemy	
			wire & trenches, many direct hits were	
			obtained & a great deal of damage done.	
	18.		8 rounds fired by Y. 47" T M Bty on enemy	
			wire.	
	19		15 rounds fired by Y. 47" T M Bty on enemy wire	
			28 " " " Z " " " " "	
			trenches, considerable damage was done.	
	20		47" Divisional Trench Mortars Camp	
			moved from Roclincourt to camp off the	
			Arras – Bailleul main road. H.1.C.8.8.	
	21		Work continued on new pits.	
	22		"	
	23		"	

A6945 Wt. W11422/M1160 350,000 12/16 D. D. & L. Forms/C./2118/14.

Instructions regarding War Diaries and Intelligence Summaries are contained in F. S. Regs., Part II. and the Staff Manual respectively. Title pages will be prepared in manuscript.

WAR DIARY
or
INTELLIGENCE SUMMARY.
(*Erase heading not required.*)

Army Form C. 2118.

4.

Place	Date	Hour	Summary of Events and Information	Remarks and references to Appendices
Oppy Wood and Gavrelle Sectors	October 24.		3 rounds fired by Z 4" T M Bty on enemy's wire	
	25		21 rounds fired by Y. 4" T M Bty on enemy's wire & trenches considerable damage was done	
	26.		25 rounds fired by Y. 4" T M Bty on enemy's trenches	
			One 6" Newton Mortar conveyed by G.S. wagon from 4" Div A R P to Y. 4" T. M. B at Gavrelle.	
			8 rounds were fired by Z 4" T M Bty in retaliation for enemy's firing on Oppy Wood.	
	27/28.		Nil rounds fired work continued	
	29		100 rounds of 6" T.M. ammunition sent	

A6945 Wt. W11422/M1160 350,000 12/16 D. D. & L. Forms/C./2118/14.

Instructions regarding War Diaries and Intelligence Summaries are contained in F. S. Regs., Part II. and the Staff Manual respectively. Title pages will be prepared in manuscript.

WAR DIARY
or
INTELLIGENCE SUMMARY.
(*Erase heading not required.*)

Army Form C. 2118.

5

Place	Date	Hour	Summary of Events and Information	Remarks and references to Appendices
Oppy Wood and Gavrelle Sectors	Oct.		up by G.S. wagon from 47 Div. S.A.A. to X/47 T.M. Bty at Gavrelle	
	30.		Y fired 12 rounds of 2" on enemy's wire. A 6" Newton mortar was fired by Y. 47 T.M.B. for the first time in the 47 Division. 30 rounds were fired & considerable damage was done.	
	~~31~~.		2 guns 6" mortars were sent up to Z 47 T.M. Bty.	
	31.		16 rounds 2" were fired by Y Bty & also 20 rounds of 6". Z Bty fired 25. 3. 6" Newton mortars were sent up by G.S. wagon to Y Bty. 200 rounds were sent up by railway to Z 47 T.M. Bty.	

[signature] Captain
D.T.M.O. 47th Division.

A6945 Wt. W11422/M1160 35,000 12/16 D. D. & L. Forms/C./2118/14.

WAR DIARY 47th Div. Arty. T.M.B's

or

~~**INTELLIGENCE**~~ **SUMMARY.**

(Erase heading not required.)

Army Form C. 2118.

(1) November 1917

Vol 25

Instructions regarding War Diaries and Intelligence Summaries are contained in F. S. Regs., Part II. and the Staff Manual respectively. Title pages will be prepared in manuscript.

Place	Date NOV. 1917	Hour	Summary of Events and Information	Remarks and references to Appendices
Arras Front	1.		20 rounds of 6" fired by Y 47th T.M.B. on enemy's wire & trenches, satisfactory results obtained	
	2.		33 rounds of 6" fired by Y 47th T.M.Bty on enemy Trench Mortars	
	3.		44 rounds of 6" fired by Y 47th T.M.Bty on enemy's defences & in retaliation to enemy's T. mortars.	
			3 rounds fired by Z 47th T.M.Bty in registration	
			2/Lt J.D. Marriage & No. 43085 Corpl G. Greave of Y 47th T.M.Bty wounded.	
	4.		X 47 T.M.Bty fired 56 rounds 6"	
			Y " " " 74 "	
			Z " " " 96 "	
			V " " " 65 "	
			A raid was carried out by 47th Div Infantry Trench Mortars fired a smoke barrage to conceal the advance of the Infantry	

A6945 Wt. W11422/M1160 350,000 12/16 D. D. & L. Forms/C./2118/14.

Instructions regarding War Diaries and Intelligence Summaries are contained in F. S. Regs., Par. II. and the Staff Manual respectively. Title pages will be prepared in manuscript.

WAR DIARY
or
INTELLIGENCE SUMMARY.
(Erase heading not required.)

(2)

Army Form C. 2118.

Place	Date	Hour	Summary of Events and Information	Remarks and references to Appendices
	Nov 1917			
Arras	4		The raid was successful 19 prisoners being	
Front			captured also 4 machine guns & 2 Light	
			Trench Mortars	
			No 63992 Bdr G. T. Orme of V. 47th T M Bty was	
			killed in action	
	5		Nil rounds fired	
	6		" " "	
	7		" " "	
	8		73 rounds of 6" fired by V 47th T M Bty on enemy T Ms	
	9		18 " " " " " " " " "	
	10		18 " " " " " " " " "	
	11		6 " " " " " " " "	
	12		8 " " " " " " " "	
			90 " " Z " "	
			Very satisfactory results were obtained	
			on all the above shoots	

Instructions regarding War Diaries and Intelligence Summaries are contained in F. S. Regs., Part II, and the Staff Manual respectively. Title pages will be prepared in manuscript.

WAR DIARY
or
INTELLIGENCE SUMMARY.
(Erase heading not required.)

(3)

Army Form C. 2118.

Place	Date	Hour	Summary of Events and Information	Remarks and references to Appendices
	NOV 1917			
Arras Front	13		18 rounds of 6" fired by 2/47th T.M. Bty on enemy defences	
	14		Work carried out on new positions	
	15		" " " " "	
	16		27 rounds of 6" fired by 2/47th T.M. Bty on enemy's defences	
			& in retaliation to enemy T.Ms.	
	17		Work continued on new positions	
	18		" " " " "	
	19		" " " " "	
	20		" " " " "	
	21		47th Div T. Mortars relieved by 21st Div. T. Mortars	
			47th Div T.M's moved camp & personnel by lorries	
			from Arras-Beaulieu road to Estree Cauchie	
	22.		Stayed at Estree Cauchie	
	23		Moved by road from Estree Cauchie to Wanquetin	
	24		" " " Wanquetin to Boisleux	
			St Marc.	

A6945 Wt. W11422/M1160 350,000 12/16 D. D. & L. Forms/C./2118/14.

Instructions regarding War Diaries and Intelligence Summaries are contained in F. S. Regs., Part II. and the Staff Manual respectively. Title pages will be prepared in manuscript.

WAR DIARY
or
INTELLIGENCE SUMMARY.
(*Erase heading not required.*)

Army Form C. 2118.

(14)

Place	Date	Hour	Summary of Events and Information	Remarks and references to Appendices
	Nov			
Arras	1917			
Front.	25		Moved by lorries from Bouleux St Marc to Bus	
	26		Stayed in billets at Bus	
	27		"	
	28		"	
	29		Moved from Bus by road to L'Ecluse	
	30		Stayed in billets at L'Ecluse	

[signature]
Captain.
D.A.D.M.O. 47th (London) Division.

A6945 Wt. W11422/M1160 350,000 12/16 D. D. & L. Forms/C./2118/14.

Instructions regarding War Diaries and Intelligence Summaries are contained in F. S. Regs., Part II. and the Staff Manual respectively. Title pages will be prepared in manuscript.

Trench Mortar Batteries
47th Div Arty

WAR DIARY
or
~~INTELLIGENCE SUMMARY.~~
(Erase heading not required.)

T M Bty
December 1917
Vol 26

Army Form C. 2118.

Place	Date December	Hour	Summary of Events and Information	Remarks and references to Appendices
HAVRINCOURT				
	1.		47th Div T M Camp at Village of L'Echelle moved to Aerodrome outside L'Echelle	
	2		Training carried out	
	3		" " "	
	4		" " "	
	5		" " "	
	6		" " "	
	7.		" " "	
	8.		All Batteries proceeded up the line to bury Dead Horse in & near Havrincourt	
	9		" " " " "	
	10		" " " " "	
	11		" " " " "	
	12.		2/47th T M Battery proceeded up the line to build defensive 6" T M positions	
	13.		Work continued on positions.	

Instructions regarding War Diaries and Intelligence Summaries are contained in F. S. Regs., Par. II. and the Staff Manual respectively. Title pages will be prepared in manuscript.

WAR DIARY
or
INTELLIGENCE SUMMARY.
(*Erase heading not required.*)

Army Form C. 2118.

Place	Date	Hour	Summary of Events and Information	Remarks and references to Appendices
HAVRINCOURT	December 1917			
	14.		Work continued on positions	
	15		Capt J.G. Brown MC D.T.M.O. 47th Divn proceeded on leave	2/Lt.
	16		A.C. Peacock MC took over duties of D.T.M.O.	
	17		Work continued on "new" positions	
	18.		Y.47th T.M.B. relieve 2/47th T.M.B. in the line.	
	19.		Work continued on positions.	
	20.		2 positions completed & 2 6" T.M's put in	
	21		New positions started	
	22		" " "	
	23		" " "	
	24		" " "	
	25.		" "	
	26.		X/47th T.M.B. relieved Y.47th T.M.B. in the line.	
	27		Work continued on positions	
	28		12 6" Mortar positions selected for defensive purposes covering Divl front	
	29		Work commenced on new positions.	

A6945 Wt. W11422/M1160 350,000 12/16 D. D. & L. Forms/C./2118/14.

Instructions regarding War Diaries and Intelligence Summaries are contained in F. S. Regs., Par. II. and the Staff Manual respectively. Title pages will be prepared in manuscript.

WAR DIARY
or
INTELLIGENCE SUMMARY.
(Erase heading not required.)

Army Form C. 2118.

Place	Date	Hour	Summary of Events and Information	Remarks and references to Appendices
	December 1917			
HAVRINCOURT.				
	30.		47th Divl. T M Camp moved from Aerodrome near L'Echelle to camp on the Neuville Fins main Road.	
			12 6" T. Mortars & 1. 9. 45" T. M. taken over from 59th Divl. T. Mortars	
	31.		Work continued on new pits	

[illegible] Lieut.
D. T. M. O. 47th Division

47 D T M Bty

Vol 27

Army Form C. 2118.

Instructions regarding War Diaries and Intelligence Summaries are contained in F. S. Regs., Part II. and the Staff Manual respectively. Title pages will be prepared in manuscript.

WAR DIARY
or
INTELLIGENCE SUMMARY.

(Erase heading not required.)

Place	Date	Hour	Summary of Events and Information	Remarks and references to Appendices
CAMBRAI SECTOR	Jan 1918 1		Work continued on new positions. No. 696969 Gunner Jones G. T. of V. 47 T.M. Bty was killed in action.	
	2		Work continued on new pits.	
	3		47th Divl T. Mortar camp moved from Neuville to Havrincourt Wood. On arrival at new camp, wagons, mules & personnel were heavily bombed by enemy aircraft. The following casualties occurred:	
			No. 951350 Bdr. Atkins [illegible] X 47 T.M. B. killed	
			" 956511 Gr Harrison [illegible] do do wounded	
			" 20606 " Gill H. do do do	
			" 960717 " Blake G. T. do do do	
			" 961685 Bdr Valentine H. do do do	
			" 960318 Corpl Gibbons J. G. Z do do do	
			" 956127 Gr Stevenson J. Y do do do	
			6 of the mules were killed & 4 of the wagons were blown up & the Corpl in charge of the team & 3 drivers were wounded. A new camp was eventually found in Havrincourt Wood.	
	4		Work continued on pits. No 971546 Gr [illegible] of X 47th T M Bty wounded.	

(A7092). Wt. W12839/M1293. 750,000. 1/17. D. D. & L., Ltd. Forms/C.2118/14.

Instructions regarding War Diaries and Intelligence Summaries are contained in F. S. Regs., Part II. and the Staff Manual respectively. Title pages will be prepared in manuscript.

WAR DIARY
or
INTELLIGENCE SUMMARY.
(Erase heading not required.)

Army Form C. 2118.

(2)

Place	Date	Hour	Summary of Events and Information	Remarks and references to Appendices
	January 1918			
Cambrai Sector	5.		Work continued on positions	
	6		do do do	
	7		2. 6" Newton mortars sent up to 2/47th [illegible] & got into action.	
	8		4. 6" Newton mortars in the line handed over to D.T.M.O. 17th Division. D.T.M.O. 17th Division sent 4. 6" mortars to our Corps camp to replace these.	
	9		3 more 6" Newton mortars sent up to 2/47 [illegible]	
	10.		Work continued & 3 more guns were put into action	
	11.		108 rounds of 6" fired by 247 [illegible]	
	12.		Work continued on new positions	
	13.		do do do	
	14.		Y. 47th T.M. Bty relieved X. 47th T.M. Bty in the line	
	15.		3. rounds fired by Z/47th T.M. Bty [illegible]	
	16.		Work started on offensive positions	
	17		do do do	
	18.		10 rounds fired by X. 47th T.M. Bty [illegible] enemy defences.	
	19.		25 rounds fired by X. 47th T.M. Bty on enemy defences [illegible] retaliation by the enemy on the village of [illegible]	

(A7092). Wt. W12839/M1293. 750,000. 1/17. D. D. & L., Ltd. Forms/C.2118/14.

Instructions regarding War Diaries and Intelligence Summaries are contained in F. S. Regs., Part II. and the Staff Manual respectively. Title pages will be prepared in manuscript.

WAR DIARY
or
INTELLIGENCE SUMMARY.
(Erase heading not required.)

(3)

Army Form C. 2118.

Place	Date	Hour	Summary of Events and Information	Remarks and references to Appendices
			January 1918.	
[illegible] Sector	20.		Work continued on dug-outs [illegible]	
	21		do do do do	
	22		do do do do	
	23.		6 rounds fired by 2 47th T.M. [illegible] dugouts.	
			The enemy heavily [illegible] & [illegible]	
			of X 47th T.M. Bty with [illegible]	
			The following casualties [illegible]	
			2/Lieut. M. G. Black X/47th T.M. Bty [illegible]	
			979951 Bdr. Binstead F. do do	do
			951261 Gr. [illegible] do do	do
			971510 [illegible] do do	do
			970131 [illegible] do do	do
			971481 Jones A. S. do do	do
			160726 [illegible] do do	do
			970293 [illegible] do do	do
			150290 [illegible] do do	do
	24		[illegible]	
			The [illegible] with [illegible] & the following	
			casualties occurred	
			67127 Corpl. [illegible] X/47th [illegible]	
			20695 Gr. [illegible] do do do	
			961201 [illegible] do do do	
			965553 [illegible] do do	

(A7092). Wt. W12839/M1293. 750,000. 1/17. D. D. & L., Ltd. Forms/C.2118/14.

Instructions regarding War Diaries and Intelligence Summaries are contained in F. S. Regs., Part II. and the Staff Manual respectively. Title pages will be prepared in manuscript.

WAR DIARY
or
INTELLIGENCE SUMMARY.
(Erase heading not required.)

Army Form C. 2118.

(4)

Place	Date	Hour	Summary of Events and Information	Remarks and references to Appendices
	January 1918			
[illegible]	25.		The enemy again bombarded 47 [illegible] dug outs [illegible] the following casualties occurred	
			951554 Bdr Carmichael 47" T.M.B. Gassed	
			950865 Gnr [illegible] H do do do	
			137315 " Harrold J do do do	
			966645 [illegible] G do do do	
			144965 Williamson W do do do	
	26		8 rounds fired by 2 47" T.M.B. on enemy defences	
	27/28		Work carried on defensive positions	
	28		45 rounds fired by 2 47" T.M.B. on enemy's defences.	
	29		60 do do do do do	
	30		96 do do do do do	
	31		54 do do do do do	

J. S. [illegible]

[illegible] Capt [illegible]

D.T.M.O. 47th Division

Instructions regarding War Diaries and Intelligence Summaries are contained in F. S. Regs., Part II. and the Staff Manual respectively. Title pages will be prepared in manuscript.

WAR DIARY
or
INTELLIGENCE SUMMARY.
(*Erase heading not required.*)

47 D TM Btt (1)

Army Form C. 2118.

Vol 28

Place	Date	Hour	Summary of Events and Information	Remarks and references to Appendices
CAMBRAI SECTOR	Feb 1918.			
	1.		87 rounds of 6" T.M. ammunition fired by X/47th T.M.B on enemy's defences. Slight retaliation by the enemy.	
	2.		7 rounds fired by Z. 47th T.M. Bty.	
	3.		Work on new positions started by Y & Z. 47th T.M. B's.	
	4.		36 rounds fired by Z 47th T.M.B. on enemy machine gun emplacements. 1. machine gun emplacement completely destroyed.	
	5.		Work continued on new positions	
	6		do do do	
	7.		do do do	
	8.		19 rounds fired by Z. 47th T.M.B on enemy defences.	
	9.		Work continued on new position by both T.M. Batteries.	

Instructions regarding War Diaries and Intelligence Summaries are contained in F. S. Regs., Part II. and the Staff Manual respectively. Title pages will be prepared in manuscript.

WAR DIARY
or
INTELLIGENCE SUMMARY.
(Erase heading not required.)

Army Form C. 2118.

(2)

Place	Date	Hour	Summary of Events and Information	Remarks and references to Appendices
CAMBRAI SECTOR	Feb 1918.			
	10.		43. rounds fired by X.47th T.M.B. in retaliation to enemy shelling our front line with light Trench Mortars.	
	11.		8. rounds fired by X.47th T.M.B. on enemy defences.	
	12		Work continued on new positions	
	13		do do do do	
	14.		do do do do	
	15.		3 rounds fired by X.47th T.M.B in registration of new gun.	
	16.		Enemy shelled X.47th T.M.B. dugouts with Gas shells. the following casualties occurred. 970132. Cpl. Dixon. A. Gassed. 950490. Gnr. Jones E Gassed. 831204 Gnr. Burston. A Gassed. 631651 Gr Jackson W. Gassed	

T2134. Wt. W708—776. 500000. 4/15. Sir J. C. & S.

Instructions regarding War Diaries and Intelligence Summaries are contained in F. S. Regs., Part II. and the Staff Manual respectively. Title pages will be prepared in manuscript.

WAR DIARY
or
INTELLIGENCE SUMMARY.
(Erase heading not required.)

(3)

Army Form C. 2118.

Place	Date	Hour	Summary of Events and Information	Remarks and references to Appendices
CAMBRAI SECTOR	Feb 1918			
	17.		19 rounds fired by Z. 47th T.M.B. on enemy defences. Slight retaliation by the enemy. 169803. Gnr. Broadley. A. Z. 47th T.M.B. slightly wounded.	
			Reorganisation of 47th Divisional Trench Mortars. 2. 6-gun 6" T.M. Batteries were formed. Z. 47th T.M.B. renamed X. 47th T.M.B.	
	18.		18 rounds fired by X. 47th T.M.B. on enemy defences.	
	19		55 " " " " " " "	
			12 " " " Y " " "	
	20		13 " " " Y " " "	
	21		11 " " " X " " "	
	22.		Work continued on new positions	
	23		" " " " "	
	24		Front line positions in Flesquieres	

T2134. Wt. W708–776. 500000. 4/15. Sir J. C. & S.

Instructions regarding War Diaries and Intelligence Summaries are contained in F. S. Regs., Part II. and the Staff Manual respectively. Title pages will be prepared in manuscript.

WAR DIARY
or
INTELLIGENCE SUMMARY.
(Erase heading not required.)

(4)

Army Form C. 2118.

Place	Date	Hour	Summary of Events and Information	Remarks and references to Appendices
CAMBRAI SECTOR	Feb 1918		& Ribecourt handed over to 63rd (R.N.) Divisional Trench Mortars.	
			47th Divisional Trench Mortars take over defensive mortars from 2nd & 17th Div. T.M's in METZ. TRESCAULT & HERMIES. & HAVRINCOURT.	
			2/Lt. A.P. Hawkins X 47th T.M.B. admitted to Hospital suffering from effects of Gas.	
	25.		Work started on completion of defensive positions by X & Y 47th T.M.B.	
	26		do do do do do	
			No. 64167. Cpl Collins. G. X 47th T.M.B & 78139 Gnr. Halstead. A X 47th T.M.B. wounded on their way to HAVRINCOURT.	

Instructions regarding War Diaries and Intelligence Summaries are contained in F. S. Regs., Part II. and the Staff Manual respectively. Title pages will be prepared in manuscript.

WAR DIARY
or
INTELLIGENCE SUMMARY.
(Erase heading not required.)

Army Form C. 2118.

5

Place	Date	Hour	Summary of Events and Information	Remarks and references to Appendices
CAMBRAI SECTOR	Feb 1918			
	27.		Work continued on defensive position	
	28		do do do do	
			J. G. Brown. Captain	
			D. T. M. O. 47th (London) Division	

T2134. Wt. W708–776. 500000. 4/15. Sir J. C. & S.

WAR
DIARY

47th DIVISIONAL TRENCH MORTAR BATTERIES.

M A R C H

1 9 1 8

Instructions regarding War Diaries and Intelligence Summaries are contained in F. S. Regs., Part II. and the Staff Manual respectively. Title pages will be prepared in manuscript.

WAR DIARY
or
~~INTELLIGENCE SUMMARY.~~ 47 Division T.M. Bs

(Erase heading not required.)

Army Form C. 2118.

VR 29

Place	Date	Hour	Summary of Events and Information	Remarks and references to Appendices
HAVRINCOURT WOOD	1st 3.18		Work continued on defensive mortar position in METZ HAVRINCOURT HERMIES. 100 rds per mortar sent up	
	4.3.18		47 Div T.M. Bs relieved by 19th Div TMBs in defensive positions. TMBs on relief proceeded to RIBEMONT sur L'ANCRE	
	5.3.18		Y47 TMB sent to BUS to experiment with 6" mortar mounted on railway truck	
RIBEMONT	7.3.18		"Laying" Drill & Box respirator drill carried out daily till March 21st	2 Lt English posted Y47 TMB
	21.3.18			2 Lt Paul Y47 TMB
BUS	21.3.18		Relief of 2nd Div TMBs on WELSH Ridge cancelled on account of enemy offensive	
			47 Div TMBs remained at BUS till ordered to move to H.Q.D.47 [?] afternoon of 23.3.18	
	23.3.18		3. 15 pdr BL guns destroyed at BUS. 8 6" mortars buried at NEUVILLE [?]. 4 6" mortars buried at BUS.	
		6pm	Orders were received to report to O.C. 141 Brigade for a quarry at W4D near MESNIL EN ARROUAISE for work on new RED LINE	
		7pm	Top of quarry found to be held by enemy. Withdrawal continued at 9pm as troops on right appeared to be withdrawing on SAILLY SAILLISEL	
	24.3.18		Withdrawal continued via GUILLEMONT - LONGUEVAL - BAZENTIN-LE-PETIT - CONTALMAISON - LA BOISSELLE - ALBERT to MÉAULTE. Billeted at church Army hut. 2 Lt S.S. ENGLISH wounded	
	25.3.18		Wagon obtained for rations from Reserve Supply ALBERT station. Efforts made to comply with orders to get in touch with 2nd DAC reported withdrawing to CONTAY via VILLE & LAVIEVILLE	
MÉAULTE	26.3.18		Withdrawal continued owing to enemy pressure and shelling of MÉAULTE via DERNANCOURT - BUIRE - LAVIEVILLE - HENENCOURT - WARLOY BAILLON to CONTAY	

D. D. & L., London, E.C.
(A8004) Wt. W1771/M2 31 750,000 5/17 Sch. 52 Forms/C2118/14

Instructions regarding War Diaries and Intelligence Summaries are contained in F. S. Regs., Part II, and the Staff Manual respectively. Title pages will be prepared in manuscript.

WAR DIARY
or
INTELLIGENCE SUMMARY.
(Erase heading not required.)

Army Form C. 2118.

Place	Date	Hour	Summary of Events and Information	Remarks and references to Appendices
CONTAY	26.3.18		Billetted, rations drawn from reserve supply of 3rd D.A.C. Report received from batman who had been sent to LE TRANSLOY with officers kit & officers that all had been abandoned on road owing to lack of transport	
	27.3.18		Efforts made to get in touch with D.A by continuing march via TOUTENCOURT - LEALVILLERS - LOUVENCOURT - VAUCHELLES to MARIEUX. D.A. H.Q. found at LOUVENCOURT. No accommodation in village owing to advent of Australian Division. Rations drawn by car from 4th Corps supply officer at AUTHIEULE.	
MARIEUX	28.3.18		Rested at MARIEUX	
	29.3.18		Instructions received from D.A. to get in touch with No 4 Section DAC at PUCHEVILLERS at 8 am. On arrival in village found section on the move for HERISSART	
HERISSART			Billeted. Ration drawn from No 3 Section Div Train	
	28.3.18		Instructions received to send 2 officers 60 ORs to report to O.C. 41st Brigade SENLIS for work on Battery positions	
"	29.3.18 30.3.18 31.3.18		Rest at HERISSART	

J. J. Moore Capt.
O.C. No 47 [illegible]

D. D. & L., London, E.C.
(A7883) Wt. W809/M1672 350,000 4/17 Sch. 52a Forms/C/2118/14

WAR DIARY

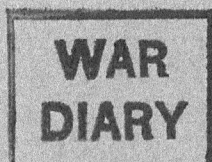

47th DIVISIONAL TRENCH MORTARS.

A P R I L

1 9 1 8

Instructions regarding War Diaries and Intelligence Summaries are contained in F. S. Regs., Part II. and the Staff Manual respectively. Title pages will be prepared in manuscript.

WAR DIARY
or
INTELLIGENCE SUMMARY.
(Erase heading not required.) 47th Divisional Trench Mortars

Army Form C. 2118.

(1) Vol 30

Place	Date	Hour	Summary of Events and Information	Remarks and references to Appendices
	APRIL.		1918	
MARTINSART.	1.		2 officers + 60. ORs of 47th Divisional Trench Mortars start building gun positions + shelters for the 47th Div Arty at SENLIS. This party carried on with this work until the 8. April 1918.	
	2.		Divisional front reconnoitred by D. T.M.O. 47th Division	
	3.		do do do do do	
	4		do do do do do	
	5.		Orders received from H.Q. 47th D.A. to put 6" T.M's in action at MARTINSART to fire on AVELUY WOOD.	
	6.		6" T.M. taken to MARTINSART. (NORTHUMBERLAND AVENUE).	
	7.		Bed for 6" T.M. + 80 rounds of 6" T.M. ammunition sent to Northumberland Avenue.	
	8.		X/47th T.M.B. relieved Y/47th T.M. Bty in the line.	
	9.		Work continued on mortar positions at MARTINSART CHATEAU + NORTHUMBERLAND AVENUE. 80 rounds of 6" T.M. ammunition sent to MARTINSART CHATEAU	
	10.		Work continued on positions.	

A5834 Wt. W4973/M687 750,000 8/16 D. D. & L. Ltd. Forms/C.2118/13.

Army Form C. 2118.

Instructions regarding War Diaries and Intelligence Summaries are contained in F. S. Regs., Part II. and the Staff Manual respectively. Title pages will be prepared in manuscript.

WAR DIARY
or
INTELLIGENCE SUMMARY.
(Erase heading not required.)

(2)

Place	Date APRIL	Hour 1918	Summary of Events and Information	Remarks and references to Appendices
MARTINSART.	10.		40 rounds fired by X/47th T M Bty on Aveluy Wood.	
	11.		3 do do do do do.	
	12.		Work continued on positions.	
	13.		47th Divisional Trench Mortars relieved by 35th Divisional Trench Mortars moved by Motor Lorries to BOUFFLERS.	
	14		Training carried out at BOUFFLERS.	
	14		do do do	
	15			
	16		do do do	
	17			
	18		do do do	
	19			
	20		do do do	
	21		do do do	
	22		do	
	23.		do. do do	
	24		do do do	
	25		do do do	
	26		do do do	
	27		do do do	
	28.		47th Divisional Trench Mortars moved by G.S. wagons to YVRENCH.	

A5834 Wt. W4973/M687 750,000 8/16 D. D. & L. Ltd. Forms/C.2118/13.

Instructions regarding War Diaries and Intelligence Summaries are contained in F. S. Regs., Part II. and the Staff Manual respectively. Title pages will be prepared in manuscript.

Army Form C. 2118.

WAR DIARY
or
INTELLIGENCE SUMMARY.
(Erase heading not required.)

(3)

Place	Date	Hour	Summary of Events and Information	Remarks and references to Appendices
	APRIL		1918	
YVRENCH	29		Training carried out at YVRENCH	
	30		do do do	

H. Brown
Captain
D. A. D. M. O. 47th Division

A5834 Wt. W4973/M687 750,000 8/16 D. D. & L. Ltd. Forms/C.2118/13.

Instructions regarding War Diaries and Intelligence Summaries are contained in F. S. Regs., Part II. and the Staff Manual respectively. Title pages will be prepared in manuscript.

WAR DIARY
or
INTELLIGENCE SUMMARY.
(Erase heading not required.)

Army Form C. 2118.

D.T.M.O. 47TH (LONDON) DIVISION. No. 1 Date ......

Vol 31

Place	Date	Hour	Summary of Events and Information	Remarks and references to Appendices
YVRENCH	1918 May 1		Training carried out while at Rest in YVRENCH	
	2		do do do	
	3		47th Div. M.T.M's. moved by lorries from YVRENCH to COUIN	
	4		Training carried out at Couin	
	5		do do do	
	6		Kits & guns etc moved by lorries from Couin to Varloy. Personnel marched.	
	7		47th Div. T.M's relieved 18th Div. T.M's in Millencourt Sector. 3. 6" T.M's taken over	
	8		Y & X. 47 T.M.B's. started work on positions	
	9		30 rounds fired by Y 47th T.M.B in S.O.S Call	
	10		Work on positions cont'd	
	11		do do do	
	12		240 rounds of 6" T.M.G. sent to both Batteries in the line	
	13			
	14		work on positions continued	
	15		do do do	
	16		Y. 47th T.M.B fired 97 rounds on enemy Trenches. X 47 T.M.B fired 15 rounds on enemy M.G. position. direct hits were obtained on both targets. Slight retaliation by the enemy	

D. D. & L., London, E.C. (A8004) Wt W1771/M2031 750,000 5/17 Sch. 52 Forms/C2118/14

Instructions regarding War Diaries and Intelligence Summaries are contained in F. S. Regs., Part II. and the Staff Manual respectively. Title pages will be prepared in manuscript.

WAR DIARY
or
INTELLIGENCE SUMMARY.
(Erase heading not required.)

Army Form C. 2118.

D.T.M.O.
47TH
(LONDON) DIVISION.
No. 2
Date ....

Place	Date (~~April~~ May)	Hour	Summary of Events and Information	Remarks and references to Appendices
			1918	
MILLENCOURT.	17.		47th Div. T.Ms relieved by 58th Div. T.M. in the Millencourt Sector. Both Batteries returned to Rest Billets at Warloy during Corps Reserve.	
	18.		47th Div. T.Ms start building defensive positions in Henencourt Wood.	
	19.		Work continued on positions. 40 rounds 6" T.M.G. sent up to positions in Henencourt Wood	
	20		Work continued on positions	
	21		do do do	
	22			
	23		do do do	
	24		do do do	
	25			
	26		do do do	
	27		do do do	
			do do do	
	28.		47th Divisional T.Ms relieved 18th Div. T.Ms. in Albert-Dernancourt Sector. 5 mortars taken over	
	29.		240 rounds of 6" T.M.G. sent up the line.	

D. D. & L., London, E.C. (A8004) Wt W1771/M2031 750,000 5/17 Sch. 52 Forms/C2118/14

Instructions regarding War Diaries and Intelligence Summaries are contained in F. S. Regs., Part II. and the Staff Manual respectively. Title pages will be prepared in manuscript.

WAR DIARY
or
INTELLIGENCE SUMMARY.

(*Erase heading not required.*)

D.T.M.O., 47TH (LONDON) DIVISION. No. 3 Date ....

Army Form C. 2118.

Place	Date	Hour	Summary of Events and Information	Remarks and references to Appendices
	~~April~~ May 1918.			
ALBERT DERNANCOURT SECTOR.	30		Y. 47th T.M. Bty fired 50 rounds on enemy M.G. + trenches. X " " 30 " " " " " Direct hits were obtained. Slight retaliation by the enemy.	
	31.		Y. 47th T.M.B. fired 22 rounds on enemy trenches. 240 rounds of 6" T.M.G. were sent up the line. 47th D.A. decided to have 10 6" T.M. in action on Divl Front with 200 rounds at each position. 7 Guns are in action on the Divl Front at present.	

J.H. Ayres.
Captain
D.T.M.O. 47th Division

D. D. & L., London, E.C.
(A8004) Wt W1771/M2031 750,000 5/17 Sch. 52 Forms/C2118/14

Instructions regarding War Diaries and Intelligence Summaries are contained in F. S. Regs., Part II. and the Staff Manual respectively. Title pages will be prepared in manuscript.

WAR DIARY
or
~~INTELLIGENCE~~ SUMMARY.
(*Erase heading not required.*)

D.T.M.O. 47TH (LONDON) DIVISION. No. 1 Date. Army Form C. 2118.

Place	Date	Hour	Summary of Events and Information	Remarks and references to Appendices
	June 1918			Vol 3
DERNANCOURT	1		X. 47th T.M. B. fired 35 rounds on enemy trenches.	
	2.		" " " 10 " " " "	
			Y " " 113 " " " "	
			Slight retaliation by the enemy.	
			288 rounds of 6" T.M. ammunition taken up to Gun positions by 47th D.A.C.	
	3.		X. Bty fired 47 rounds on M. G. positions	
			Y " " 53 " " " "	
			Enemy retaliated with a few 4.2s & light minnenwerfers	
	4.		X Bty fired 67 rounds in retaliation to hostile T.M. fire.	
			Y. Bty fired 28 rounds on Hostile T.M. positions	
			Enemy's T.M. ceased firing on commencement of our retaliatory fire	
			288 rounds of 6" T.M.G. taken up to Gun positions by 47th D.A.C.	
	5.		X. Bty fired 53 rounds on Quarry at E.14.C. (Sheet 62 D. N.E)	
			Y. " " 62 " " T.M. emplacements at E.8.B.3600	
			& E.8.B. 30 70. (Sheet 62 D NE)	
			Enemy retaliated with a few 4.2s & granatenwerfers	

D. D. & L., London, E.C. (A8004) Wt W1771/M2031 750,000 5/17 Sch. 52 Forms/C2118/14

Instructions regarding War Diaries and Intelligence Summaries are contained in F. S. Regs., Part II. and the Staff Manual respectively. Title pages will be prepared in manuscript.

WAR DIARY
or
INTELLIGENCE SUMMARY.
(Erase heading not required.)

D.T.M.O. 47TH (LONDON) DIVISION. No. 2

Army Form C. 2118.

Place	Date	Hour	Summary of Events and Information	Remarks and references to Appendices
	June 1918			
DERNANCOURT	6		Y T.M.B. fired 45 rounds on Quarry E.14.C	All Map References quoted in this War Diary refer to sheet 62D N.E.
			X " " 47 " " Hostile T.M. emplacements at E.8.B.35.00 & E.8.B.30.40.	
			Slight retaliation by the enemy.	
			288 rounds 6" T.M.G taken up to gun positions by 47th D.A.C [?]	
	7		Y Bty fired 41 rounds on Quarry at E.14.C. & on tracks in E.14.C & E.13.D.	
			X Bty 22 rounds in harassing fire at night on tracks in E.13.D & hostile M.G. emplacement E.14.C.64	
	8		X Bty fired 71 rounds on E.13.D.6.2. E.13.D.4.6.	
			Y " " 128 " " quarry & bank E14C	
			Hostile M.G. emplacement E.14.B.0.2 & in harassing fire at night on tracks E.13.D.	
			Enemy retaliated with 20 rounds of granatenwerfer.	
			No.971409 Bdr. Sabin W. X 47th T.M.B. was gassed	
			No.76320 Gr. Freedman W. Y do " wounded	
			" 965833 " Kirby W.J. Y do " do.	

D. D. & L., London, E.C. (A8004) Wt W1771/M2031 750,000 5/17 Sch. 52 Forms/C2118/14

Instructions regarding War Diaries and Intelligence Summaries are contained in F. S. Regs., Part II. and the Staff Manual respectively. Title pages will be prepared in manuscript.

WAR DIARY
or
INTELLIGENCE SUMMARY.
(Erase heading not required.)

D.T.M.O.
47TH
(LONDON) DIVISION.
No. 3/1
Date

Army Form C. 2118.

Place	Date	Hour	Summary of Events and Information	Remarks and references to Appendices
	June 1918			
DERNANCOURT	9		X. Bty fired 11 rounds in registration	
			Y " " 112 " on enemy front line from E 14 a 2560	
			to E14a 5095. & on group of granatenwerfers at	
			E.14.a.8.9	
			7101781. Gnr. Grillon. H.L. of 47th T.M.B died of wounds	
			received in action	
	10.		X. Bty fired 45 rounds on trenches running south from E 8.C	
			Y " " 86 " " " " "	
	11		X. Bty " 275 } in conjunction with raid on the	
			Y " " 97 }	
			right of Divisional front. A large dump of	
			granatenwerfers was blown up about E.14.b.7.8	
			by our T.M. fire	
			There was only slight retaliation to our fire	Sheet 62 D NE
	12.		X. Bty fired 167 rounds in retaliation to hostile T.M. fire	
			& on wire in E.8.C	
			Y. Bty fired 88 rounds on HQs. & bank in E8B.41.8	
			bank in E.13.C.	
	13		X Bty fired 167 rounds on wire & trench running S. from E 8.C	
			Y " " 76 " " "	
			E.14.a.1.3	

D. D. & L., London, E.C.
(A8004) Wt W1771/M2031 750,000 5/17 Sch. 52 Forms/C2118/14

Instructions regarding War Diaries and Intelligence Summaries are contained in F. S. Regs., Part II. and the Staff Manual respectively. Title pages will be prepared in manuscript.

WAR DIARY
or
INTELLIGENCE SUMMARY.
(Erase heading not required.)

D.T.M.O. 47TH (LONDON) DIVISION. No. 4 Date ......

Army Form C. 2118.

Place	Date	Hour	Summary of Events and Information	Remarks and references to Appendices
	June		1918	
	14		X Bty fired 42 rounds on wire & trench E 8 C	
			Y " " 121 " " " " E 14 a & Quarry	
			& Bank E. 14. C	
			very slight retaliation	
			300 rounds 6" L.M.G. sent up to gun positions	Map
	15		X Bty fired 65 rounds on wire	62^D N E
			Y " " 56	
			Enemy replied to our wire cutting with a few 4.2	
	16		X Bty fired 121 rounds on Bank & front line posts E 13 D	
			Y " " 105 " " front line wire between E. 14 a. 40.42 &	
			E 14. a 64. 94.	
			During shoot a hostile T.M. was active on our trenches, on	
			our T.Ms firing a few rounds on the suspected	
			emplacement it ceased firing	
	17		X Bty fired 113 rounds on wire & trenches running from	
			E. 14 a 40 42 to E 14 a 66 94	
			Y Bty fired 69 rounds on Bank & front line in E. 13 D	
	18		X Bty fired 114 during raid on trenches in E. 14 a	
			Y " " 118 " " " " " &	
			on E. 14. C 4. 8. Enemy was seen to retire hastily	
			from this point.	

D. D. & L., London, E.C. (A8004) Wt W1771/M2031 750,000 5/17 Sch. 52 Forms/C2118/14

Instructions regarding War Diaries and Intelligence Summaries are contained in F. S. Regs., Part II. and the Staff Manual respectively. Title pages will be prepared in manuscript.

WAR DIARY
or
INTELLIGENCE SUMMARY.
(Erase heading not required.)

D.T.M.O.
47TH
(LONDON) DIVISION.
No. 5

Army Form C. 2118.

Place	Date	Hour	Summary of Events and Information	Remarks and references to Appendices
	June 1918			
	19.		X. Bty fired 10 rounds on Quarry in E.14.C.	
			Y " " " " Bank E.13.D	
	20.		47th Divisional Trench Mortars relieved by 58th Divisional Trench Mortars & proceeded by lorries to Longpré les Amiens	
	21		Training carried out at Longpré Les Amiens.	
	22		" " " " "	
	23		" " " " "	
	24		" " " " "	
	25		" " " " "	
	26			
	27			
	28		X. 47th T.M.B. reported for duty to 235 Bde. R.F.A	
	29		Y Bty continue training	
	30		"	

J. S. Brown.
Captain
D.T.M.O. 47th Division

D. D. & L., London, E.C.
(A8004) Wt W1771/M2031 750,000 5/17 Sch. 52 Forms/C2118/14

Instructions regarding War Diaries and Intelligence Summaries are contained in F. S. Regs., Part II. and the Staff Manual respectively. Title pages will be prepared in manuscript.

WAR DIARY
or
INTELLIGENCE SUMMARY.
(*Erase heading not required.*)

Army Form C. 2118.

VR 33

Place	Date	Hour	Summary of Events and Information	Remarks and references to Appendices
	JULY.		1918.	
LONGPRÉ.	1.		Training carried out as usual	
	2.		do do do	
	3			
	4.		do do do	
	5.		do do do	
	6.		X 47th T.M.B. returned from 235 Brigade R.F.A.	
	7.		Training carried out as usual	
	8.		do do do	
	9.		do do do	
	10.		do do do	
	11.		X & Y. 47th T.M.Bs reported to 47th D.A.C. for fatigues.	
	12.		do do do do	
			do do do do	
	13.		47th Divl. T. Mortars moved by Lorries from Longpré to Warloy	
	14.		Relieved 18th Divl. T. Mortars. 6. 6" T.Ms. taken over in the Albert Sector. 4. 6" T.Ms. taken over in reserve covering Henencourt. 2. 6" T.Ms taken over at Rest billets at Warloy.	
	15.		X. Bty sent into the Line. Y. Bty. man reserve positions at Henencourt.	

D. D. & L., London, E.C. (A8004) Wt W1771/M2031 750,000 5/17 Sch. 52 Forms/C2118/14

Instructions regarding War Diaries and Intelligence Summaries are contained in F. S. Regs., Part II. and the Staff Manual respectively. Title pages will be prepared in manuscript.

WAR DIARY
or
INTELLIGENCE SUMMARY.
(Erase heading not required.)

Army Form C. 2118.

Place	Date	Hour	Summary of Events and Information	Remarks and references to Appendices
	JULY.		1918.	
ALBERT	15.		X.47th T.M.B. fired 40 rounds on enemy trenches.	
SECTOR.	16.		X " " 20 " wire & Quarry in W.27.c & Front Line W.27.a. Slight retaliation by the enemy. 300 rounds of 6" T.M. ammunition sent up the Line	All map References referred to SPECIAL
	17.		X.47th T.M.B. fired 62 rounds in retaliation to Minenwerfer firing on our trenches in W.21.C. Enemy ceased firing on our retaliation	SHEET OF SENLIS
	18.		X.47th T.M.B. fired 101 rounds in night harassing fire on Quarry at W.27.B.8.8. & wire W.21.D.25.60 & W.21.D.4.8.	PART OF
	19.		X.47th T.M.B. fired 41 rounds on H.Q. & minenwerfer position about W.27.B.6.2 & Quarry at W.27.C.2.8. No retaliation by the enemy. 300 rounds of 6" T.M. ammunition sent up the line	57D S.W. & S.E. 62D N.W. N.E.
	20.		X.47th T.M.B. fired 66 rounds on Quarry W.27.C.2.8. & in retaliation to minenwerfers in W.15.D & W.22.a & on Machine Gun post. W.27.C.65.80.	
	21.		X.47th T.M.B. fired 237 rounds in night harassing fire on Tracks in W.22.a. Trench Mortar position & Brick-works W.22.a & Tracks W.27.B.96.90 & W.15.C.90.70.	

D. D. & L., London, E.C. (A8004) Wt W1771/M2031 750,000 5/17 Sch. 52 Forms/C2118/14

Instructions regarding War Diaries and Intelligence Summaries are contained in F. S. Regs., Part II. and the Staff Manual respectively. Title pages will be prepared in manuscript.

WAR DIARY
or
INTELLIGENCE SUMMARY.
(Erase heading not required.)

D.T.M.O.
47TH
(LONDON) DIVISION.
No. 3
Date.

Army Form C. 2118.

Place	Date	Hour	Summary of Events and Information	Remarks and references to Appendices
	JULY.		1918	
ALBERT SECTOR	22.		Y. 47th T.M.B. relieved X. 47th T.M.B in ALBERT SECTOR. X. 47th T.M.B took over Reserve positions in HENENCOURT	
	23.		Y 47th T.M.B. fired 20 rounds on Sunken Rd & Wire W.21.D. 15.25.	
	24		Y. 47th T.M.B. fired 105 rounds in barraging enemy trenches in W.21 C & D during raid made by 47th Dwl Infantry on enemy trenches in W.21 D & also on Machine Gun position in W.27. C. Very slight retaliation by the enemy	
	25.		Y/47th T.M.B fired 90 Rounds during raid on W.21.D + W. 22 c. W.27.D + W. 27. C. Heavy retaliation by the enemy, on front line + supports during our bombardment.	
	26		Y/47th T.M.B. fired 45 Rounds on Sunken Road, Quarry and Trench, Mortars, in W.27.B + on trench in W.27.D 2.7.	
	27.		Y/47th T.M.B. fired 28 Rounds on Sunken Road + on enemy Trench Mortars positions in W.27 B.	

D. D. & L., London, E.C.
(A8004) Wt W1771/M2031 750,000 5/17 Sch. 52 Forms/C2118/14

Instructions regarding War Diaries and Intelligence Summaries are contained in F. S. Regs., Part II. and the Staff Manual respectively. Title pages will be prepared in manuscript.

WAR DIARY
or
INTELLIGENCE SUMMARY.
(Erase heading not required.)

D.T.M.O.
47TH
(LONDON) DIVISION.
No. 4
Date

Army Form C. 2118.

Place	Date	Hour	Summary of Events and Information	Remarks and references to Appendices
ALBERT SECTOR	JULY 28th		X/47th T. M. B. relieved Y/47th T. M. B. in the line. Y/47th T. M. B. took over Reserve positions in Aveluy[?]court.	
			X/47th T. M. Bty fired 21 rounds registration of S.O.S. lines and of Machine Gun positions W. 21. D. 2.8.	
	29th		X/47th T. M. B. fired 51 Rounds on M. G. position in W. 21. D. 2.8 & wire about W. 21. d. 45.95. A great deal of wire & wooden stakes was "put up". Enemy T. M's were very active during the night.	
	30th		X/47th T. M. Bty fired 54 rounds during Corps Artillery bombardment on the following targets. Quarry W. 27 B., M. G. & trench W. 21. D. 2.8. Minenwerfer positions W. 27. B. 4-7. Dugouts W. 27 B. 95.95.	
			Infantry report M. G. post & trench & wire in W. 21. D. 2.8. are much damaged. There was no sign of the enemy there. Slight retaliation by the enemy.	

D. D. & L., London, E.C.
(A8004) Wt. W1771/M2731 750,000 5/17 Sch. 52 Forms/C2118/14

Instructions regarding War Diaries and Intelligence Summaries are contained in F. S. Regs., Part II. and the Staff Manual respectively. Title pages will be prepared in manuscript.

WAR DIARY
or
INTELLIGENCE SUMMARY.
(Erase heading not required.)

D.T.M.O.
47TH
(LONDON) DIVISION.
No. 5
Date..........

Army Form C. 2118.

Place	Date	Hour	Summary of Events and Information	Remarks and references to Appendices
ALBERT SECTOR	JULY 31st		X/47. T. M. Battery fired 10 rounds in retaliation at 12:45 pm on Minenwerfer position in W. 27.B. Twenty five rounds were fired at 3 pm in retaliation, on position in W. 27.D. + Quarry W. 27.B. At 12:45 pm the enemy fired about 7 light Minenwerfer bombs on Swan Trench in W. 27A. Enemy was active with Granatenwerfer + Light Minenwerfer at 3pm, on trenches in W. 26 B + W. 26 C.	

J. G. Brown
Captain
D. T. M. O. 47th Division

D. D. & L., London, E.C.
(A8004) Wt. W1771/M2131 750,000 5/17 Sch. 52 Forms/C2118/14

47th Divl. Artillery

D. T. M. O.

47th DIVISIONAL TRENCH MORTARS,

AUGUST 1918.

Instructions regarding War Diaries and Intelligence Summaries are contained in F. S. Regs., Part II. and the Staff Manual respectively. Title pages will be prepared in manuscript.

WAR DIARY
or
INTELLIGENCE SUMMARY.
(Erase heading not required.)

Army Form C. 2118.

D.T.M.O. 47TH (LONDON) DIVISION. No. 1 Date 1-9-18

VR 34

Place	Date	Hour	Summary of Events and Information	Remarks and references to Appendices
	August 1918			
ALBERT SECTOR	1.		X/47th T.M.B. fired 24 rounds in registration " " " 155 " " conjunction with raid by 14th Div. Infantry from 9.10 p. to 9.35 pm. Heavy retaliation by the enemy on front line & support trenches.	
	2.		X/47th T.M. Bty fired 18 rounds on Quarry in 10.2.4.c 300 rounds 6" T.M.G. taken to the line by 47th Div	
	3.		Owing to enemy retirement in this sector, 6" T.M.B.s of 47th Division, also owing to lack of transport mortars could not be taken forward.	
	4		Y/47th T.M. Bty relieved X/47th T.M. Bty in the line	
	5.		Work commenced on strengthening of emplacements & collecting & putting in dumps of ammunition	
	6		do do do do	
	7		do do do do	
	8		do do do do	
	9		X/47th T.M.B. relieved Y/47th T.M.B. in the line	
	10		Clearing up of pits &c continued	
	11		do do do do	
	12		do do do do	

D. D. & L., London, E.C. (A8004) Wt W1771/M2031 750,000 5/17 Sch. 52 Forms/C2118/14

Instructions regarding War Diaries and Intelligence Summaries are contained in F. S. Regs., Part II. and the Staff Manual respectively. Title pages will be prepared in manuscript.

WAR DIARY
or
INTELLIGENCE SUMMARY.
(Erase heading not required.)

D.T.M.O.
47TH
(LONDON) DIVISION.
No. 2
Date 1.9.18.

Army Form C. 2118.

Place	Date	Hour	Summary of Events and Information	Remarks and references to Appendices
	August		1918	
ALBERT.	13.		Work continued on pits etc	
SECTOR.	14.		do — do — do	
	15.		X/47th T.M. Bty relieved Y/47th T.M. Bty in the line. Capt. J.G. Brown. M.C. D.T.M.O. 47th (London) Division proceeded to 4th Army Trench Mortar School. Capt. J.G. Blaver O.C. X/47th T.M.B. took over duties of D.T.M.O.	
	16		Work continued on clearing up etc.	
	17		do — do — do	
	18		do — do — do	
	19		do — do — do	
	20.		Positions started on the Albert Bouzincourt Rd Albert Millencourt Rd & in the Railway cutting near Albert	
	21.		Work continued. X Bty relieved Y Bty in the line	
	22.		X Bty fired 150 rounds on Albert before the attack. Heavy retaliation by the enemy, who obtained direct hits on the pits on the Albert Millencourt Rd & Albert Bouzincourt Rd	

D. D. & L., London, E.C.
(A8004) Wt W1771/M2031 750,000 5/17 Sch. 52 Forms/C2118/14

Instructions regarding War Diaries and Intelligence Summaries are contained in F. S. Regs., Part II. and the Staff Manual respectively. Title pages will be prepared in manuscript.

WAR DIARY
or
INTELLIGENCE SUMMARY.
(*Erase heading not required.*)

D.T.M.O. 47TH (LONDON) DIVISION. No. 3 Date 1.9.18

Army Form C. 2118.

Place	Date	Hour	Summary of Events and Information	Remarks and references to Appendices
	August 1918			
ALBERT SECTOR	22		50 rounds were destroyed by enemy shell fire.	
	23.		6" T.M. Bs out of action owing to enemy retirement.	
	24.		2 guns taken up to ~~Becourt~~ BECOURT Wood but owing to the rapidity of enemy retirement by the time the positions were dug the enemy was out of range	
	25.		Clearing up of position started	
	26.		1 N.C.O & 20 men sent to work on ammunition dump on Albert Fricourt road	
	27		Rest Billets moved from Warloy to former Bty H.Q.s in W 20 c off the Albert Bouzincourt Road.	

D. D. & L., London, E.C. (A8004) Wt W1771/M2031 750,000 5/17 Sch. 52 Forms/C2118/14

Instructions regarding War Diaries and Intelligence Summaries are contained in F. S. Regs., Part II. and the Staff Manual respectively. Title pages will be prepared in manuscript.

WAR DIARY
or
INTELLIGENCE SUMMARY.
(Erase heading not required.)

D.T.M.O. 47TH (LONDON) DIVISION. No. 4 Date 1.9.18

Army Form C. 2118.

Place	Date	Hour	Summary of Events and Information	Remarks and references to Appendices
	August 1918			
ALBERT	28		Training carried out at Rest Billets	
SECTOR	29		do do do	
	30		do do do	
	31		do do do	

J. Hase
Captain R.F.A.
a/D.T.M.O. 47th Division

D. D. & L., London, E.C. (A8004) Wt W1771/M2031 750,000 5/17 Sch. 52 Forms/C2118/14

WAR DIARY
or
INTELLIGENCE SUMMARY.
(Erase heading not required.)

Instructions regarding War Diaries and Intelligence Summaries are contained in F. S. Regs., Part II. and the Staff Manual respectively. Title pages will be prepared in manuscript.

Army Form C. 2118.

D.T.M.O., 47TH (LONDON) DIVISION. No. 1 Date 1-10-18.

Vol 35

Place	Date	Hour	Summary of Events and Information	Remarks and references to Appendices
	September 1918			
BOUZINCOURT.	1.		Training carried out as usual	
	2.		47th Div. T. Mortars marched from Bouzincourt to Fricourt Wood.	
			Capt. J.G. Brown M.C. D.T.M.O. 47th Division returned from 4th Army T.M. School.	
	3.		Stayed at Fricourt Wood.	
	4.		Camp moved from Fricourt Wood to camp on MONTAUBAN - MARICOURT ROAD.	
	5.		Stayed at MONTAUBAN Camp.	
MONTAUBAN.	6.		2 6" mobile Trench Mortars sent up the line at PRIEZ FARM, but owing to caterpillars these were brought back to camp.	
	7.		47th Divl Trench Mortars marched from MONTAUBAN CAMP to MERICOURT.	
	8.		Captain J.G. Brown M.C. D.T.M.O. 47th Division proceeded on leave & Capt. J.G. Blaver took over duties of D.T.M.O.	

D. D. & L., London, E.C. (A8004) Wt W1771/M2031 750,000 5/17 Sch. 52 Forms/C2118/14

Instructions regarding War Diaries and Intelligence Summaries are contained in F. S. Regs., Part II. and the Staff Manual respectively. Title pages will be prepared in manuscript.

WAR DIARY
or
INTELLIGENCE SUMMARY.
(*Erase heading not required.*)

D.T.M.O.
47TH
(LON[illegible]) DIVISION.
No. 2
Date

Army Form C. 2118.

Place	Date	Hour	Summary of Events and Information	Remarks and references to Appendices
	September.			
MERICOURT.	8.		47th Div. T. Mortars entrained at MERICOURT.	
	9.		do do ~~discen~~ detrained at LILLERS and	
BELLERY.			marched to BELLERY.	
	10.		Training carried out at BELLERY.	
	11.		do do do	
	12		do do do	
	13.		do do do	
	14		do do do	
	15		do do do	
	16		do do do	
	17		do do do	
	18		do do do	
	19.		do do do	
			do do do	
	20.		47th Divl. T. Mortars marched from BELLERY to FAUX	
FAUX.			near PERNES.	
	21		Training carried out at FAUX	
	22		do do do	
	23		do do do	
	24		do do do.	

D. D. & L., London, E.C.
(A8004) Wt W1771/M2031 750,000 5/17 Sch. 52 Forms/C2118/14

Instructions regarding War Diaries and Intelligence Summaries are contained in F. S. Regs., Part II. and the Staff Manual respectively. Title pages will be prepared in manuscript.

D.T.M.O.
47TH
(LONDON) DIVISION.
No. 3
Date ———

Army Form C. 2118.

WAR DIARY
or
INTELLIGENCE SUMMARY.
(Erase heading not required.)

Place	Date	Hour	Summary of Events and Information	Remarks and references to Appendices
	September 1918			
FAUX	25		Training carried out at Faux	
	26		do do do Capt. J. G. Brown M.C. D.T.M.O. 47 Div returned from leave.	
	27		do do do	
FLEURY	28		47th Div T. Mortars marched from FAUX to FLEURY	
	29		Training carried out at FLEURY	
	30		do do do	

J. G. Brown
Captain
D.T.M.O. 47th Division

D. D. & L., London, E.C.
(A8004) Wt W1771/M2031 750,000 5/17 Sch. 52 Forms/C2118/14

Instructions regarding War Diaries and Intelligence Summaries are contained in F. S. Regs., Part II. and the Staff Manual respectively. Title pages will be prepared in manuscript.

WAR DIARY
or
INTELLIGENCE SUMMARY.

(Erase heading not required.) 47th Divisional Trench Mortars

D.T.M.O. 47TH (LONDON) DIVISION.

Army Form C. 2118.

40 36

Place	Date	Hour	Summary of Events and Information	Remarks and references to Appendices
	OCTOBER 1918			
	1		47th Divl Trench Mortars moved from FLEURY to BELLERY.	
	2		47th Divl Trench Mortars moved from BELLERY to ROBECK.	
	3		47th Divisional T Mortars moved from ROBECK to LA GORGUE.	
	4		47th Divl T. Mortars moved from LA GORGUE to MASSELOT POST near LAVENTIE.	
RADINGHAM			Relieved 59th Divl T Mortars in the line at RADINGHEM.	
	5		2 guns sent up the line to X/47th T.M. Bty. Capt. J.G. Brown M.C. Gen List D.T.M.O. 47th Divn reported MISSING. Capt. J.G. Blaver O.C. X/47th T.M.B. assumed command of 47th Divl T Mortars	

Instructions regarding War Diaries and Intelligence Summaries are contained in F. S. Regs., Part II. and the Staff Manual respectively. Title pages will be prepared in manuscript.

WAR DIARY
or
INTELLIGENCE SUMMARY. 2
(Erase heading not required.)

D.T.M.O. 47TH (LONDON) DIVISION. No. .... Date ....

Army Form C. 2118.

Place	Date	Hour	Summary of Events and Information	Remarks and references to Appendices
	October		1918	
Radinghem	6		2 Guns sent to 1/47 T.M.B. in the line.	
	7		work continued on positions	
	8.		1/47 T.M.B. went into the line & took 4 6" Trench Mortars	
	9		work continued on positions	
	10		95 rounds fired on wire & M.G. positions in conjunction with raid	
			450 rounds sent up the line	
	11		26 rounds fired on wire	
	12		work continued on positions	
	13		40 rounds fired on wire & enemy trenches Slight retaliation by the enemy with light Trench Mortars.	
	14		32 rounds fired on wire	
			250 " " in conjunction with raid on enemy trenches carried out by 142nd Inf. Brigade	

D. D. & L., London, E.C.
(A8004) Wt W1771/M2031 750,000 5/17 Sch. 52 Forms/C2118/14

Instructions regarding War Diaries and Intelligence Summaries are contained in F. S. Regs., Part II. and the Staff Manual respectively. Title pages will be prepared in manuscript.

WAR DIARY
or
INTELLIGENCE SUMMARY. 3

(*Erase heading not required.*)

Army Form C. 2118.

Place	Date	Hour	Summary of Events and Information	Remarks and references to Appendices
			October 1918	
Radinghem	15		Work continued in the line	
			2 6" T Ms mobile went into action near Fort [illegible] and	
	[illegible]		fired 20 rounds on enemy M.G. post	
			All guns brought out of the line to	
	17.		Rest Billets	
	18.		47th Divl Trench Mortars moved by lorries to St. FLORIS	
			Training carried out at ST. FLORIS	
	19		do do do	
	20			
	21		do do do	
	22			
	23		do do do	
	24		do do do	
	[illegible]		do do do	
	25.		47th Divl Trench Mortars moved from St. FLORIS to HAUBORDIN	
	26		Training carried out at HAUBORDIN	
	27		do do do	

D. D. & L., London, E.C. (A8004) Wt W1771/M2031 750,000 5/17 Sch. 52 Forms/C2118/14

Instructions regarding War Diaries and Intelligence Summaries are contained in F. S. Regs., Part II. and the Staff Manual respectively. Title pages will be prepared in manuscript.

WAR DIARY
or
INTELLIGENCE SUMMARY.
(Erase heading not required.)

(4)

D.T.M.O., 47TH (LONDON) DIVISION. No. .... Date ....

Army Form C. 2118.

Place	Date	Hour	Summary of Events and Information	Remarks and references to Appendices
			October 1918	
	28		47th Divl T Mortars moved from HAUBORDIN to BREUCQ	
	29		Training carried out at BREUCQ	
	30		do — do — do	
	31.		47th Divl T Mortars moved from BREUCQ to BLAINDAIN & relieved the 57th Divl T Mortars.	

[illegible]
Captain R.F.A.
A/D. T. M. O. 47th Division

Instructions regarding War Diaries and Intelligence Summaries are contained in F. S. Regs., Part II. and the Staff Manual respectively. Title pages will be prepared in manuscript.

WAR DIARY
or
INTELLIGENCE SUMMARY.
(Erase heading not required.) 47th Divisional Trench Mortars

Army Form C. 2118.

VIII 37

Place	Date	Hour	Summary of Events and Information	Remarks and references to Appendices
	November 1918.			
PONT. A. CHIN and FROYENNES.	1.		Work on positions continued.	MAPS SHEET. 37 France
	2.		Y. 47th T.M.B. fired 40 rounds on machine gun post. No. 920817 Corpl. Pike G. T. Y. 47th T.M.B. wounded & this N.C.O. died of wounds 3.11.18.	
	3.		Y. 47th T.M.B. fired 35 rounds on movement in Houses in I 33 a & C.	
	4.		Y. 47th T.M.B. fired 51 rounds on machine gun post in I 33	
	5.		53 rounds fired by X. 47th T.M.B. in retaliation to enemy Trench Mortar fire & on machine gun at O.15.D.4.3.	
	6.		46 rounds fired by Y. 47th T.M.B on machine gun & Trench Mortars in I 27 & I 33.	
	7		Nil rounds fired, clearing up of pits etc	
	8		do do do	
	9		do do do	
	10.		do do do	
	11.		do do do Armistice signed & took effect as from 11.00 hours.	

D. D. & L., London, E.C. (A8004) Wt W1771/M2031 750,000 5/17 Sch. 52 Forms/C2118/14

Instructions regarding War Diaries and Intelligence Summaries are contained in F. S. Regs., Part II. and the Staff Manual respectively. Title pages will be prepared in manuscript.

WAR DIARY
or
INTELLIGENCE SUMMARY.

(Erase heading not required.) 47th Divl. Trench Mortars

D.T.M.O., 47TH (LONDON) DIVISION. No. 2 Date 1.12.18.

Army Form C. 2118.

Place	Date	Hour	Summary of Events and Information	Remarks and references to Appendices
	November		1918.	
Templeuve.	12.		All. 6" T. Mortars. taken out of the line & brought to Rest Billets at Templeuve.	
	13		Training carried out at Templeuve	
	14.		—do —do —do.	
	15.		47th Divl. Trench Mortars marched from Templeuve to Bourghelles.	
	16.		Training carried out at Bourghelles.	
	17.		47th Divl. Trench Mortars moved to Cysoing.	
	18		Training carried out at Cysoing	
	19			
	20			
	21			
	22			
	23		—do —do —do.	
	24			
	25			
	26.			

D. D. & L., London, E.C. (A8004) Wt W1771/M2031 750,000 5/17 Sch. 52 Forms/C2118/14

Army Form C. 2118.

WAR DIARY
or
INTELLIGENCE SUMMARY.
(*Erase heading not required.*) 47th Divl. Trench Mortars

Instructions regarding War Diaries and Intelligence Summaries are contained in F. S. Regs., Part II. and the Staff Manual respectively. Title pages will be prepared in manuscript.

Place	Date	Hour	Summary of Events and Information	Remarks and references to Appendices
	November		1918	
✝	27.		47th Divl. Trench Mortars marched to FOURNES.	
	28.		" " " " " La Beuvrière.	
	29		" " " " " Fouquereuil.	
	30.		Training carried out at Fouquereuil	

J. F. Hasel[?]

Captain R.F.A.

D.T.M.O. 47th Division

D. D. & L., London, E.C.
(A5004) Wt W1771/M2031 750,000 5/17 Sch. 52 Forms/C2118/14

Instructions regarding War Diaries and Intelligence Summaries are contained in F. S. Regs., Part II. and the Staff Manual respectively. Title pages will be prepared in manuscript.

WAR DIARY
or
INTELLIGENCE SUMMARY.
(Erase heading not required.)

D.T.M.O., 47TH (LONDON) DIVISION. No. 1. Date 1-1-19.

Army Form C. 2118.

983

Place	Date	Hour	Summary of Events and Information	Remarks and references to Appendices
	December 1918.			
FOUQUEREUIL.	1.		Training & Educational Scheme carried out at FOUQUEREUIL.	
	2. 3. 4. 5. 6. 7. 8.		— do — do — do — do.	
LABEUVRIERE.	9.		47th Divisional Trench Mortars move from FOUQUEREUIL to LABEUVRIERE.	
	10.		Training & Educational Scheme carried out at LABEUVRIERE.	
	11.		— do — do — do.	
	12.		20 O.Rs. sent to 235 Bde. R.F.A. for work on huts etc.	
	13		Training & Educational Scheme carried out at LABEUVRIERE.	
	14.		— do — do — do	
	15.		— do — do — do	

D. D. & L., London, E.C. (A8004) Wt W1771/M2031 750,000 5/17 Sch. 52 Forms/C2118/14

Instructions regarding War Diaries and Intelligence Summaries are contained in F. S. Regs., Part II. and the Staff Manual respectively. Title pages will be prepared in manuscript.

WAR DIARY
or
INTELLIGENCE SUMMARY.
(Erase heading not required.)

D.T.M.O. 47TH (LONDON) DIVISION. No. 2 Date 1.1.19.

Army Form C. 2118.

Place	Date	Hour	Summary of Events and Information	Remarks and references to Appendices
	December 1918.			
LABEUVRIERE.	16.		20. ORs. sent to 236. Bde. R.F.A. for work on Huts etc.	
	17		Training & Educational Scheme carried out.	
	18			
	19			
	20		—do —do —do	
	21			
	22			
	23			
	24.		All detached. Trench Mortar personnel returned to Unit.	
	25.		X-mas Dinner & Concert.	
	26.		20 ORs sent to 235 Bde. R.F.A. & 20 ORs to 236 Bde. R.F.A.	
	27.		Training carried out.	
	28.		1. Officer & 20 ORs sent to work at Y.M.C.A. BETHUNE.	
	29.		5 ORs. sent to R.T.O. BETHUNE. for Police Duties	
	30. 31.		Training carried out	

J. S. Haves
Captain. R.F.A.
D.T.M.O. 47th Division

D. D. & L., London, E.C. (A8004) Wt W1771/M2031 750,000 5/17 Sch. 52 Forms/C2118/14

Instructions regarding War Diaries and Intelligence Summaries are contained in F. S. Regs., Part II. and the Staff Manual respectively. Title pages will be prepared in manuscript.

WAR DIARY
or
INTELLIGENCE SUMMARY.
(Erase heading not required.)

Army Form C. 2118.

Vol 39

Place	Date	Hour	Summary of Events and Information	Remarks and references to Appendices
Field	1-1-19 to 22-1-19		Training and Educational Instruction	
Field	23-1-19 to 31-1-19		Attached to 47th D A C for Duty	

J. Rae[illegible]
Captain RVO

D. D. & L., London, E.C.
(A8004) Wt W1771/M2031 750,000 5/17 Sch. 52 Forms/C2118/14

www.ingramcontent.com/pod-product-compliance
Lightning Source LLC
Chambersburg PA
CBHW081538160426
43191CB00011B/1790
9781474526104